MOUNTAINS, MONSTERS, AND MERCY

A Father's Reckoning with Loss, Grit, and the Climb Back to Grace

RYAN CASTLEBERRY

For permissions and inquiries, visit RyanCastleberry.com

ISBN: Paperback: 979-8-9946368-0-0

Hardback: 979-8-9946368-1-7

Ebook: 979-8-9937548-0-2

Published in the United States

First Edition

TABLE OF CONTENTS

DEDICATION

For Madison, you are the reason I climbed when I wanted to fall. Every step, every breath, every moment of grace was for you. You are my *why*. For Chelsea, your light showed me what love could be, and your loss taught me that some things are worth carrying forever. Thank you for the gift of those days. For the TBI Community, to those navigating the invisible injuries, the struggles no one else can see: You are not broken. You are warriors on a different battlefield. Keep climbing. Your story matters. For the Veterans, brothers and sisters who know the weight of service, the cost of sacrifice, and the long road home: This climb is ours. We fall, we rise, we carry each other. Always Ready.

I was Air Force Tactical Air Control Party, attached to Army units—so my world spoke Army as much as Air Force.

And for anyone standing at the base of their own mountain, wondering if they have what it takes—you do. One step at a time. Let's climb together.

DISCLAIMER

This book is a memoir based on my personal experiences and recollections. Some names, locations, and identifying details have been changed to protect the privacy of individuals. Any resemblance to actual persons, living or dead, or actual events is purely coincidental.

The content in this book is provided for informational and inspirational purposes only. It is not intended to be a substitute for professional medical advice, diagnosis, or treatment. Always seek the advice of your physician, mental health professional, or other qualified health provider with any questions you may have regarding a medical or mental health condition.

If you are experiencing a mental health crisis or are having thoughts of self-harm, please reach out for help immediately:

- National Suicide Prevention Lifeline: 988 (call or text)
- Crisis Text Line: Text HOME to 741741
- National Alliance on Mental Illness (NAMI) Helpline: 1-800-950-NAMI (6264)
- Emergency Services: 911

The 30-Day Climb framework described in this book is based on my personal journey and should be adapted to your individual needs and circumstances. Please consult with appropriate healthcare professionals before beginning any new physical activity or making significant lifestyle changes.

The views and opinions expressed in this book are my own and do not necessarily reflect the views of any organizations, employers, or other entities mentioned or referenced.

While I have made every effort to ensure the accuracy of the information presented, I make no guarantees about the completeness, reliability, or accuracy of this information. Any action you take upon the information in this book is strictly at your own risk.

PREFACE

This book was not written from a place of perfection, but from the wreckage of my own failures, losses, and painful lessons. It is a story of survival, of facing monsters both outside and inside, of climbing mountains that seemed impossible, and of learning to extend mercy when all I wanted to do was fight.

If you are struggling to keep your head up, if you've been told you are broken, or if you've lost the ones who mattered most—this book is for you.

But I don't want you to just read my story. I want you to climb with me.

Throughout these pages, you'll find more than memories and reflections. You'll discover a framework I call the 30-Day Climb—a simple, repeatable practice designed to build momentum in your own life. Not through grand gestures or heroic efforts, but through small, consistent actions that, over time, become who you are.

The Climb isn't complicated. It follows a simple weekly progression:

- Week One → two intentional days
- Week Two → three intentional days
- Week Three → four intentional days
- Week Four → five intentional days

On those intentional days, you commit to four anchors: Movement, Reflection, Connection, and Mercy.

If you're ready to begin this journey—not just to witness mine, but to start your own—I invite you to take the Climber's Oath below. Say it aloud. Write it down. Let it be the first step of many.

The mountains won't shrink. The monsters won't disappear overnight. But with each step up the trail, you'll discover what I did: that you are stronger than you know, and that mercy—extended to yourself and others—can transform even the deepest wounds into wisdom.

Let's climb together.

THE CLIMBER'S OATH

I am not defined by my failures or my losses.
I commit to showing up, even when I don't feel like it.
I will move my body, reflect on my journey, connect with others, and extend mercy—to myself first, then to those around me.

I understand that transformation isn't built on heroic moments, but on small, consistent actions. I will climb at my own pace, without comparison or judgment. When I fall, I will get back up. When others fall, I will lend my strength. This is my climb. This is my promise.

PART ONE

TRIALS AND TRIBULATIONS

The monsters in life don't always announce themselves with roars and razor teeth. Sometimes they appear as golden arches on the horizon when your pockets are empty. Sometimes they arrive as floodwaters rising silently in the night, or as smoke seeping under a door. Sometimes they come disguised as the ordinary—a curve in the road, a phone call, a question from a child you can't answer.

These are the stories of breaking points—moments when life demanded more than I thought I could give. They were the trials that tested not just my strength or my will, but my very understanding of who I was.

In these early chapters, you'll see me at my lowest—unable to buy french fries for my daughter, standing in the wreckage of a flooded home, cradling a dog who didn't survive a fire, and learning to walk again after a motorcycle crash nearly took everything. These aren't stories of triumph. They're stories of survival, of the bare-knuckled fight to stay standing when everything within you wants to fall.

But these trials, these tribulations—they aren't the end of the story. They're the beginning. They're the foundation stones of a different kind of strength, one built not on never breaking, but on learning how to piece yourself back together when you do.

As you read these first chapters, I invite you to reflect on your own trials. Not to compare scars or to minimize your pain, but to recognize that we all face moments that feel impossible. We all encounter monsters we didn't see coming. And we all have the capacity to keep climbing, even when the mountain seems too steep.

1
FRENCH FRIES AND FRAGILE HOPE

We were driving down the road when Madison's little voice piped up from the back seat. She couldn't form long sentences yet, but her excitement was loud and clear: "French fries!"

She had spotted the golden arches rising above the tree line, and her whole face lit up. Her eyes sparkled, her body leaned forward in her car seat as if she could will us there faster.

For a split second, I wanted to match her excitement. I wanted to pull in, order her a Happy Meal, and watch her light up even more. But as reality hit, my chest tightened.

I had nothing. Not a dollar in my pocket. Not even enough change rattling around the console to buy her the smallest bag of fries.

I gripped the steering wheel tighter, my knuckles white. My mind raced for excuses, for some way to explain it. But she was too young to understand.

"I can't today," I muttered. My voice cracked, betraying the shame I felt.

Her face fell instantly. The joy drained from her eyes, replaced by confusion and then heartbreak. She screamed, fists pounding against the straps of her car seat. Tears streamed down her face, and her sobs filled the truck.

Every cry was like a blade in my chest. It wasn't about fast food. It was about failure.

I was the father who could not provide the most basic of joys—a bag of fries. I was the dad who could not say yes. At that moment, I wasn't even sure I was a dad she could count on at all.

That moment has never left me. I've carried broken bones, scars, and trauma. But nothing cracks me open like remembering the sound of her sobs and the sight of her little fists pounding the air.

Even now, years later, it's a memory that sneaks up on me. I'll be in the middle of a quiet moment, and suddenly I'll feel the weight of it again—that gut-punch realization of failing the person you love most.

It was just french fries. But it wasn't. It was the day I knew something had to change. The day I swore I'd never let her down in that way again.

Years later, I stood in my living room, phone in hand, heart hammering against my ribs.

It was Madison's birthday. She would be turning fourteen—no longer the little girl who cried over french fries, but a young woman with her own life, her own friends, her own world that increasingly didn't include me.

The distance between us had grown with each passing year. The custody arrangement, my work rotations, my own mistakes—they had all piled up into a wall that seemed too high to climb.

I had rehearsed what I would say. Simple, direct, honest: "Happy birthday, Madison. I love you. I'm here."

I dialed her number, listened to it ring. Once. Twice. Three times. Then voicemail. I tried again an hour later. Voicemail.

Again, that evening. Voicemail. I left a message the third time, my voice steadier than I felt: "Hey, Madison, it's Dad. Just wanted to wish you happy birthday. I love you. Call me if you want to talk."

She never called back. That night, I sat on my porch, staring at the silent phone. The french fries memory crashed over me again—her little voice, her excitement, her disappointment. Only now, there wasn't even a cry. Just silence. And that silence cut deeper than her sobs ever had.

I realized then that failure isn't always a single moment. Sometimes it's a pattern, a slow erosion of connection, a series of small absences that add up to something irreparable.

I still had the urge to fix it all at once—to show up with grand gestures, to make promises I wasn't sure I could keep. But I knew that wasn't the answer.

The french fries taught me about immediate failure—the sharp pain of letting someone down in a moment. The silence taught me about long-term failure—the hollow ache of relationship damaged over time.

Both lessons broke me open. Both showed me exactly who I did not want to be.

We've all had moments when we couldn't provide what someone needed from us. We've all felt that sinking realization that we've let down someone we love. It might not be french fries. It might be emotional support during a crisis, or showing up for an important event, or simply being present when someone is speaking.

The specifics don't matter. What matters is what we do after—how we respond to the knowledge of our own inadequacy. Do we hide from it? Do we make excuses? Or do we face it squarely and commit to change?

I couldn't go back and buy those french fries. I couldn't undo the patterns that had led to the birthday silence. But I could start building something new—a foundation of small, consistent actions that, over time, might rebuild trust.

That's what this book is about. Not perfection. Not heroics. Just the steady climb back toward being someone others can count on.

REFLECTION: When the Small Things Break You

It's not always the catastrophic events that break us. It's often the small, ordinary moments that shine a light on where we feel least capable.

That day in the truck was a mirror I couldn't escape. It showed me who I was—and who I didn't want to be. That's where transformation begins: not in the heroic climbs, but in the quiet humiliations that hurt the most to admit.

➤Think back on a negative or unfortunate event in your life, especially one that may not have seemed significant in itself. Did it convey an accusation or a hard lesson that impacted you? What did you do in response?

MERCY PRACTICE: The Three-Breath Reset

When shame or failure threaten to overwhelm you, try this simple practice:

1. First breath: Inhale for four counts, hold for four counts, exhale for six counts. As you exhale, name the feeling: "This is shame." "This is failure." "This is inadequacy."

2. Second breath: Inhale for four counts, hold for four counts, exhale for six counts. As you exhale, remind yourself: "I am not defined by this moment."

3. Third breath: Inhale for four counts, hold for four counts, exhale for six counts. As you exhale, ask yourself: "What is the next right step I can take?"

This isn't about erasing the feeling. It's about creating enough space to respond rather than react. Practice this whenever you feel yourself spiraling into shame or self-judgment.

The french fries moment broke me, but it wouldn't be the last time life stripped me bare. In fact, the universe was just warming up. What came next would test not just my ability to provide, but my very will to survive.

2

WHEN THE RIVER ROSE THIRTY FEET

The camper wasn't supposed to be home. It was meant for weekends and vacations—a place to rest after adventures, not a place to survive.

But after the divorce, it became my world. I had given up my Harley so my ex-wife could have a car, and the judge left me with the camper and the payments. She remarried before the ink on the papers was dry, and I was left with four walls of aluminum and silence.

Nights were long. The walls seemed to close in tighter each time I came back from rotation at the oilfield. With no family nearby and no friends checking in, I was left with myself, my failures, and the hum of the air conditioner.

I tried to keep my focus on the future. Two years into the oilfield, I had taken every course possible, working all the way through mid-supervisor training even while staying in the role of operator. I wanted to be ready—if the chance came, I would have no excuse not to take it.

Then came the hailstorm.

A Texas spring storm rolled in one night, pounding the camper like a thousand hammers. By the time it passed, the metal was dented, windows cracked, seams split. Insurance inspected it and declared it a total loss.

Strangely, I felt hopeful for once. They would cut a check, and after paying off what was owed, I'd even pocket a few thousand. Enough to get a small place. Enough to feel, for the first time in a long time, a little normal.

But twelve hours later, the river rose.

The Medina came up thirty feet in half a day, swallowing everything in its path. When I arrived at the floodplain, I stared in disbelief. The only thing left visible was the air conditioner unit on the roof. Everything else—clothes, photos, furniture, memories—was underwater.

The smell hit next: muddy, oily, a mix of sewage and rot that clung to the back of my throat like tar. It was the smell of everything wrong—organic matter decaying, chemicals leaching, and the river carrying waste from miles upstream. One breath of it and my stomach lurched. This wasn't just water damage. This was desecration.

I wanted to believe some of it could be salvaged. But when I waded closer, the reality was undeniable.

Everything was ruined.

I called insurance, confused. "The camper was already a total loss. What happens now?" They told me to go through it anyway, to make a list, to itemize what I could.

I didn't want to. Every item was a reminder of how far I had fallen. Every box of photos, every piece of clothing, every item caked in sludge was a memory stripped of its dignity.

I walked past other sites where massive fifth-wheel campers had been carried downstream and shattered against rocks. Part of me wished mine had been one of them. At least then it would have been gone—no reminder, no wreckage to sift through.

But my spot was different. Somehow, the flood had risen, destroyed everything inside, and then left the camper sitting stubbornly in place.

My kayak was still wedged under it. The beer bottle from the steak I had grilled the night before was still sitting by the chair. Everything was right where I had left it. Only now, everything was ruined.

No friends called. No family checked in. No one asked if I was okay or if I had somewhere to go.

But the company gave me a week in a hotel. For that I was grateful.

The first night in that hotel room, I stood under the shower for almost an hour. The water ran dark at first—river silt from my skin, mud from under my fingernails, grime from my hair. I watched it circle the drain, carrying away the physical evidence of what had happened, though the weight of it still pressed on my chest.

The room itself was nothing special—standard corporate lodging with beige walls, a desk that wobbled slightly, and a bed too soft for my back. But it was clean. It was dry. And for the next seven days, it was mine.

I established a routine immediately. Two alarms—one at 5:00 a.m., another at 5:05. Not because I needed the extra five minutes, but because routine meant control, and control meant survival.

Each morning, I made the bed with military precision—corners tight, pillows centered, comforter smoothed flat. The housekeepers probably thought I was strange, but it mattered to me. In a world that had just been obliterated, this small act of order was a lifeline.

I would shower, dress, and walk to the nearest café for coffee. Black, no sugar. I'd sit by the window, watching people rush to jobs, to meetings, to lives that hadn't been swallowed by water. Their normalcy felt foreign to me, like watching a movie where everyone knew the plot except me.

By day three, the insurance adjuster called. He needed that inventory list, and he needed it soon. I sat at the desk in my hotel room that evening, trying to recall every item that had been in that camper. The clothes were easy. The furniture too. But how do you inventory memories? How do you put a price tag on the only photo you had of your grandfather, now dissolved into pulp? How do you claim the value of your daughter's drawings, turned to colored mush by the flood?

I wrote until my hand cramped, the list growing longer with each remembered loss. When I couldn't write anymore, I set the pen down and looked at my hands—calloused, rough, capable of so much work, yet unable to hold onto the things that mattered most.

That night I walked down to the hotel bar. I hadn't eaten all day. I ordered a chicken quesadilla and a Corona. The bartender asked how my day was.

I bit my lip, held back the tears pressing hard against my chest, and smiled. "It'll be a good day once I have this quesadilla and this beer. I just lost everything."

She blinked, not sure how to respond. But I meant it. I was grateful for that small moment—for food, for a drink, for something that felt normal in the middle of disaster.

I carried my plate back to my room, sat by the window, and stared out at the city lights. I didn't know what tomorrow would bring. But I knew one thing: There wasn't time to sit around waiting to be rescued.

Each morning after that, I would wake up and say it out loud to the empty room: "Left foot, right foot." It became my mantra. Not inspiring, not profound, just necessary. Left foot, right foot. The simplest instruction to keep moving forward when standing still wasn't an option.

I had one week and no time to cry. No one was coming. It was up to me.

And when the week ended, I did what I always did. I handled my problems. I showed up for my next rotation.

Back at work, no one asked about the flood. No one knew. I didn't bring it up, and life at the rig continued as if nothing had happened. In a strange way, there was comfort in that routine—the familiar weight of tools in my hands, the predictable rhythm of the job, the clear expectations I could meet. Out there, I wasn't a man who had lost everything. I was just an operator doing his job. During those first weeks after the flood, I learned something that would carry me through later disasters: Control what you can, let go of what you can't.

I couldn't control the river. I couldn't control the insurance timeline. I couldn't control the fact that no one showed up to help.

But I could control how I responded. I could control the way I made my bed each morning in that hotel room. I could control showing up to work on time. I could control saying "thank you" for a quesadilla and a beer when it would have been easier to crumble.

It's a lesson I've carried through fire, through broken bones, through heartbreak. When the world is drowning you, find the one thing—however small—that you can still control. Start there. Then find another. And another.

Left foot, right foot.

Survival isn't always about grand strategy. Sometimes it's about simply taking the next step, and then the step after that, until you find yourself on dry ground again.

REFLECTION: Gratitude in Devastation

The flood stripped me bare, but it also gave me clarity.

Gratitude doesn't erase pain, but it gives you a weapon against despair. Sometimes survival isn't about climbing mountains or conquering giants. Sometimes it's about a quesadilla and a beer. Sometimes it's about finding the smallest reason to keep going until a bigger one comes along.

That week in the hotel, I learned that gratitude isn't only about appreciating blessings when life is good. It's about finding light when everything is dark. It's about holding onto one small thing and letting it be enough to carry you forward.

➤Consider a time in your life when you were crushed or had something important taken from you. What did you do? In the devastation, was there anything for which you were grateful?

MERCY PRACTICE: Control versus Let Go List

When life feels overwhelming, try this exercise to regain perspective:

1. Take a sheet of paper and draw a line down the middle.
2. On the left side write "Things I Can Control" and on the right "Things I Cannot Control."
3. List everything causing you stress, placing each item in the appropriate column.
4. For the "Cannot Control" items, write next to each: "I release this."
5. For the "Can Control" items, choose ONE to focus on today.

This practice isn't about ignoring problems; it's about directing your energy where it can actually make a difference. Even in floods—literal or metaphorical—there's always something small you can control. Start there.

I thought the flood had taught me everything I needed to know about loss. I was wrong. Two years later, I would face another kind of devastation—one that wouldn't just take my possessions, but would steal a life I loved and test the limits of what I could bear.

3
SMOKE, ASH, AND CALVIN'S LAST BREATH

The smudges on the glass weren't right.

Every day I wiped the sliding glass door clean. Calvin, Chelsea's rainbow-coated dog and my buddy, loved to sit there with his nose pressed against the glass, watching the world. His nose prints were part of the routine—my OCD tendencies made sure the glass stayed spotless, but his smudges were the exception I allowed. They were proof of life, proof of him.

But this time, they looked blackened. Something was wrong.

I pulled the door open, and it felt like stepping into a parallel universe. Everything was in place—the furniture, the pictures, the little details of life—but it was all cloaked in soot, warped by heat, and carrying a smell that hit me like a punch to the chest.

Smoke, chemicals, rot. It burned my lungs and made my head spin.

"Calvin!" I called, stumbling through the dark. The power was out, the air still thick with haze. Each step forward was a fight against the acrid air and the fear rising in my chest.

I tore through every room, eyes darting into corners, under tables. He wasn't there. My heart raced faster, pulse pounding in my ears.

Finally, in the bathroom, I found him.

Calvin was in the tub, lifeless, his nose pressed to the drain as if searching for one last pocket of clean air. My chest collapsed. My legs gave out.

I dropped to my knees beside him, numb. My hand hovered over his still body, but I couldn't bring myself to touch him. It was too final, too crushing.

I staggered back outside, choking. Chelsea was waiting, her face searching mine for hope, for something other than the truth I carried in my eyes.

"He's gone," I whispered. Her scream split the air. She tried to run past me, but I caught her, held her back as she fought against me. She pounded my chest, sobbing, demanding to see him, to make it untrue. All I could do was hold her as she collapsed in my arms, both of us broken in the parking lot while the world carried on around us.

Firefighters arrived to check for hotspots. They confirmed what we already knew—the fire was out, but the damage was done. Later I found out the neighbor upstairs had felt his floor getting hot but dismissed it. Another neighbor thought she had left a curling iron plugged in but decided not to worry. The indifference stung almost as much as the flames.

During the renovation, one neighbor even complained about construction noise starting too early in the mornings. I wanted to scream at her, "Oh, how inconvenient for you! I lost everything! And Calvin died in that fire."

But I didn't. I swallowed the words, letting them burn in my throat. That night, we had nowhere to go. We called people we thought we could lean on, but one told us flatly, "Tonight's not a good night."

I hung up the phone, stunned. You're right, I thought. I just lost everything. Again. Tonight isn't a good night.

Finally, another neighbor took pity and found us a place to stay for the night. It wasn't home, but at least it was somewhere.

Not one family member called. Not one friend checked in. No one showed up with dinner, no one asked if we needed clothes, no one offered even the smallest gesture of care.

It was Calvin and me. And now it was just me. I didn't know how to process the grief, so I did what I always did: I buried it under work, under grind, under the relentless voice inside me that said, "Handle your problems. Nobody's coming. Keep moving."

Three weeks later, Chelsea and I stood in what remained of our living room. The renovation crew had begun the process of gutting the place, stripping away the smoke-damaged drywall and melted fixtures. The chemical smell still hung in the air, fainter now but persistent.

"They're letting us take a few things," I told her. "If there's anything salvageable."

We moved through the space like ghosts, touching nothing at first, just looking at the ruin of what had been our home. The couch where we'd curled up, watching movies. The kitchen where we'd cooked together. The spot by the window where Calvin would sit for hours, watching birds and squirrels with intense focus.

"The couch," Chelsea said finally, breaking the silence. "Maybe we can save the couch."

I looked at it—stained with soot, smelling of smoke, its fabric singed in places. But the frame was intact. The cushions could be replaced.

"We'll take it," I told the crew chief. "We'll clean it up."

He looked dubious but nodded. Two workers helped me carry it outside and load it onto my truck. It was a small victory in a sea of loss, but it mattered. Not because we needed a couch, but because we needed something—anything—that survived.

That night, we sat on the bare frame of that couch in our temporary lodging, drinking beer and not saying much. The silence between us was heavy, loaded with grief for Calvin, anger at the neighbors, fear of what came next.

"I keep thinking I hear him," Chelsea said finally. "His nails on the floor. The jingle of his collar." I nodded. I'd been hearing it too. Phantom sounds of a life that was gone.

"I know it's stupid," she continued, "but I keep wondering if he was scared. If he was looking for us."

I reached for her hand, held it tight. There were no words for this kind of pain. Nothing I could say would make it better. So I just held on, anchoring her in the storm of grief.

That couch became a strange symbol for us—scarred but salvageable, carrying the marks of disaster but still functional. We spent hours cleaning it, replacing cushions, treating the frame for smoke damage. When we were finally able to move back in, it was the first piece of furniture we brought inside.

It wasn't the same, of course. Nothing was. But it was something. A small continuity in a world that had been completely disrupted.

Later, when Chelsea and I would fight—about money, about the future, about the thousand small frictions that stress creates—I would sometimes look at that couch and remember the night we sat on its bare frame, holding hands in silence. How even in our worst moment, we had found a way to hold on to each other. How we had salvaged what we could from the ashes.

We've all lost companions who saw us at our worst and stayed anyway. We've all experienced that particular hollow ache of an empty bed, a missing greeting at the door, the absence of someone—human or animal—who was simply there, witnessing our lives. In those losses, we learn something about what truly matters: not the things that burn or break, but the presence that makes a house a home.

REFLECTION: Fire As Teacher

The fire stripped more than possessions. It stripped illusions.

I had believed that when disaster struck, people would show up. That family would circle the wagons, that friends would rush in. Instead, there was silence. Complaints. Indifference.

It taught me one of the hardest truths I've ever learned: Nobody is coming to save you.

Resilience is built in those moments when the world doesn't rally to your side. It's built in the silence, in the ashes, in the choice to stand back up even when no one else notices you're on the ground.

That fire didn't just burn a home. It burned away the illusion that help was guaranteed. And in that loss, it forced me to find a strength I didn't know I had—the strength to be my own rescue.

➢Have you ever gone through a particularly hard time, and the people you thought would be there, weren't; or the ones you thought would help, didn't? What did you learn from that? In such experiences, have you found or forged a new inner strength?

MERCY PRACTICE: Letter of Forgiveness

When resentment or anger threatens to consume you, try this practice:

1. Choose one person or situation connected to your pain.
2. Write a letter expressing everything you feel—the hurt, the anger, the disappointment. Don't hold back.
3. When you're done, read it aloud to yourself.
4. Then write at the bottom: "I release this burden. It is no longer mine to carry."
5. Finally, destroy the letter—burn it, tear it up, delete the file.

This isn't about excusing harmful actions or pretending you weren't hurt, and it isn't simply about venting your rage. It's about freeing yourself from the weight of carrying that pain forward. The goal isn't reconciliation with others—it's peace within yourself.

The fire had taken Calvin, nearly taken our home, and tested our relationship. But the universe wasn't done with me yet. My body, the one thing I thought I could control, would be the next battlefield—and the fight for survival would be measured not in possessions lost, but in bones broken and will tested.

4
BROKEN BONES, UNBROKEN WILL

The Harley Sportster was my pride. I'm not a big-framed guy, but on that bike I felt ten feet tall. I had taught myself to ride, gotten my license, and every time I kicked it over and pulled onto the road, I wore a grin I couldn't hide.

That day I had ridden into Helen, Georgia, to finally stop at a biker shop I had passed a hundred times. I bought a long-sleeve shirt—part souvenir, part protection. I thought it would keep me warm on cool rides. An hour later, that shirt was being cut off my body in a trauma room.

The crash itself is gone from my memory, erased by impact. Later they told me what happened. A big SUV had turned in front of us. My face smashed into the windshield, my body went over the hood. My ex wife was on the bike too—she was hurt, but my injuries were far worse. My body was a wreck.

I awoke in the hospital days later, tubes running, machines beeping, teeth gone, bones screaming. My body felt foreign, as if I had been stitched together wrong.

The damage was extensive: Crushed left orbital, two broken cheeks, broken nose and roof of my mouth completely broken in half. That made each breath a knife-stab of pain, facial fractures that left half my face numb, teeth knocked out or broken at the gum line. The doctors spoke in clinical terms about surgeries and recovery timelines. I heard them through a fog of pain medication and disbelief.

When they finally let me look in a mirror, I barely recognized myself. Swollen, bruised, cut—the face looking back at me was a stranger's. My eyes were the only thing I knew, and even they looked different, haunted by what they'd seen.

But people showed up. My gym community rallied—mowing my grass, feeding my dogs, even pooling money to keep us afloat for the first month. I'll never forget that generosity. But I also knew it wouldn't last.

So as soon as I could move, I clawed for work. Barely able to walk, I taught boot camps. I ran spin classes with my body screaming in protest. I even took on catering jobs just to put food on the table.

Every bone in my body hurt. Every step was agony.

At Sheppard Rehab, I taunted my therapist. "Is that all you've got?" I thought I was proving toughness. Really, I was masking fear.

She smiled. "I've got something for you."

Finally, I thought, *a real challenge*.

She had me stand on one leg, extend my arms, lift the other leg bent at the knee, and hold. My body trembled like a leaf in a storm. My muscles screamed. My pride collapsed.

"What the hell is this?" I gasped.

She smirked. "Welcome to Pilates. I do it five times a week."

She got me. She broke me in a way the crash hadn't. And in doing so, she built me back stronger.

I became obsessed with recovery, with testing my limits, with proving I was still whole. Each day, I'd push a little further—one more rep, one more mile, one more hour without pain meds. The physical therapists warned me to slow down, that healing couldn't be rushed. I nodded and then promptly ignored them.

This was my form of control. I couldn't control the accident. I couldn't control the pain. But I could control how hard I worked to come back.

I was told at least a year before I could ride a bicycle and I may never run again. I refused to accept that so 363days after the crash, I signed up for a sprint triathlon. It was insanity. My body was nowhere near ready. But I needed to prove something—to myself, to the world, to the fear that had taken up residence in my chest since the moment I woke up in that hospital bed.

The swim nearly broke me. Every stroke sent shockwaves through my still-healing body. By the time I dragged myself onto land, I was gasping, dizzy, on the edge of collapse.

"You can stop," a volunteer said, seeing my condition. "There's no shame in it."

But there was shame—in my mind. Stopping meant the accident had won. Stopping meant I was broken.

I got on the bike, gritting what teeth I had left. Each pedal stroke was a negotiation with pain. The run that followed was more of a shuffle, my broken ribs protesting with every footfall.

I finished dead last. But I finished.

Looking back, I recognize it now for what it was: not strength, but fear. Fear of being weak, fear of being vulnerable, fear of being left behind. I pushed my body to its breaking point because I was terrified of what it meant to be broken.

But the weight of it all didn't end in that rehab room or at that finish line. A month later, I got a call. The driver of the SUV had taken his own life.

I grieved for him, for his demons, and for his family. I grieved for the reminder that it could have been me. I had crossed paths with his story, and now he was gone. It haunted me—a reminder of how fragile the line is between surviving and surrendering.

My ex-wife tried to remind me who I was. "Any other time in life, if you had an opportunity, you always took it. You can do this too."

I didn't feel that I could. I was scared. I was broken. But I kept moving.

And then there was Buck Rogers.

My attorney's real name was Brian Rogers, but everyone called him Buck. We sat together one day as I told him how I just kept pushing forward. He leaned back, looked at me, and said, "I commend you. No matter what happens, you just keep pushing. Most people would have given up."

I laughed bitterly. "Buck, you bastard. Nobody told me I had an option!"

He chuckled, shaking his head. But that line stuck.

Later, Buck asked if he could take my bloodied helmet from the crash and turn it into a plaque. He wanted to hang it in his office.

"Why?" I asked.

"For my clients who want to quit," he said simply. "So they can see your story and know it's possible to keep going."

I didn't see myself as an inspiration. I saw myself as a man limping forward because there was no other choice. But if my broken bones, my scars, or my stubbornness could fuel someone else's fight—then maybe that pain wasn't wasted.

That crash taught me something I wish I'd known sooner: that physical strength isn't the same as resilience. I could push my body to its limits, but the true test wasn't how fast I could come back. It was whether I could accept being broken, whether I could find worth beyond physical capability, whether I could ask for help when I needed it most.

We all face moments that knock us down, that break us open, that leave us wondering if we'll ever be whole again. It might not be a motorcycle crash. It might be illness, job loss, heartbreak, or failure. The specifics don't matter. What matters is the choice we make when faced with our own fragility.

Do we deny it? Do we rage against it? Or do we find a way to move forward with it—not in spite of our brokenness, but within it?

REFLECTION: Broken Bones, Unbroken Will

Resilience isn't glamorous. It's not standing tall with a cape. It's limping forward with scars, bruises, and broken bones when no one would blame you for quitting.

Sometimes your survival isn't just about you. Sometimes it becomes the proof someone else needs that quitting isn't the only option.

My helmet still hangs on Buck's wall. To some, it's a warning. To others, it's a spark. To me, it's a reminder: I didn't stop. Even when every part of me wanted to.

➤In what way have you been broken, really broken and crushed? What did you do in response? What was the result? Were you resilient in any way? What did you learn?

MERCY PRACTICE: Endurance Mindset Exercise

When facing a difficult challenge or recovery, try this practice to build mental endurance:

1. Identify your "minimum viable success" for today. This isn't your ideal outcome—it's the absolute baseline that counts as showing up. (Example: Walking to the mailbox, making one phone call, writing one paragraph.)
2. Before beginning, ask yourself: "What will I do when it gets hard?" Plan your response to difficulty before you encounter it.
3. During the task, when resistance hits, say to yourself: "This is where I grow." Not, "This is where I quit," or even, "This is where I push through," but specifically, "This is where I *grow*."
4. After completing even the smallest success, acknowledge it specifically: "I said I would, and I did it."

This practice builds the mental muscle that turns "I can't" into "I can, even when it's hard." Use it whenever you face something that seems beyond your current capacity.

The accident had rebuilt my body, but it hadn't prepared me for what came next. Physical pain has limits, boundaries, an end point. Emotional pain is different. When Chelsea walked away, I would discover a whole new kind of brokenness—one no amount of physical rehabilitation could fix.

WEEKONEOF THE 30-DAY CLIMB

After each trial, each tribulation, I kept searching for the key that would unlock transformation. I tried white-knuckling it through pain. I tried drowning it in work. I tried ignoring it, fighting it, and running from it. None of these strategies brought lasting change.

What finally worked wasn't grand or heroic. It was simple, sustainable, and surprisingly gentle: two intentional days a week.

That's where we begin the Climb—with Week One's commitment to just two intentional days. It might not sound like enough, especially if you're coming from a place of all-or-nothing thinking. Trust me, I fought against this at first too. "Only two days? That can't possibly make a difference."

But here's what I learned: The floor matters more than the ceiling.

Think about it. What's more sustainable—a perfect week followed by burnout, or a consistent practice that gradually expands? The 30-Day Climb is built on the second approach. We start with two intentional days because almost anyone can manage two days, even in the midst of chaos.

What makes a day "intentional"? Four simple anchors:

1. MOVEMENT: Do something physical. Walk, run, lift, stretch, ride. It doesn't have to be extreme, but it has to push you out of comfort. Your body needs to remember it's alive.
2. REFLECTION: Write one page in a journal. Gratitude, pain, lessons, questions—doesn't matter. What matters is honesty. Get the thoughts out of your head and onto the page.
3. CONNECTION: Reach out to someone. A text, a call, a conversation. Don't isolate. Don't disappear. Build ties instead of walls.
4. MERCY: Give yourself grace at least once. Instead of beating yourself up, acknowledge the failure, but refuse to let shame define the day.

That's it. Four anchors. Simple. Repeatable.

Here's what a Week One tracker might look like:

WEEKONETRACKER

Days committed: two

DAY 1: ________ (date)

[ ] MOVEMENT: What I did: ________

[ ] REFLECTION: One page written

[ ] CONNECTION: Whom I reached out to: ________

[ ] MERCY: Where I extended myself grace: ________

DAY 2: ________ (date)

[ ] MOVEMENT: What I did: ________

[ ] REFLECTION: One page written

[ ] CONNECTION: Whom I reached out to: ________

[ ] MERCY: Where I extended myself grace: ________

Notes:

____

____

____

____

____

____

____

And here's a sample journal entry from my own first week of the Climb:

SAMPLE JOURNAL ENTRY - DAYONE

Today I showed up. That's it. That's the victory.
I didn't want to move. My body felt like concrete, and my mind kept finding excuses. But I committed to this. So I put on my shoes and walked to the end of the block and back. Not impressive. Not Instagram-worthy. But it counts.

I texted Mark. Just a simple "How are you doing?" He's going through his own problems right now, and I've been avoiding reaching out because I don't have solutions for him. But maybe he doesn't need solutions. Maybe he just needs to know someone remembers he exists.

As for mercy—I caught myself in the mirror today, seeing all the flaws, all the failures, all the ways I'm not who I thought I'd be at this age. The old me would have leaned into that shame spiral. Today I just said, "You're doing your best with what you have." Not perfect. Not fixed. Just trying. And for today, that's enough.

Tomorrow might be harder. Or easier. Doesn't matter. I just need to show up again.

The power of Week One isn't in intensity—it's in starting momentum. Two intentional days give you evidence that you can trust yourself. They build the foundation for everything that follows.

As you begin your own Week One, remember:

- Choose your two days in advance.
- Keep expectations realistic.
- Celebrate showing up, not just achievement.
- Trust that small actions, repeated consistently, lead to big change.

The mountains won't shrink in Week One. The monsters won't disappear. But you'll prove to yourself that you can take two steps forward, even when the trail seems impossibly steep.

The accident broke my body, and recovery rebuilt it, but that didn't prepared me for what came next. Physical pain has limits, boundaries, an end point. Emotional pain is different. When Chelsea walked away, I would discover a whole new kind of brokenness—one no amount of physical rehabilitation could fix.

PART TWO

LOVE AND LOSS

There's a particular kind of pain that comes with watching someone walk away—whether it's a lover whose laughter once filled your home or a child whose hand once reached for yours without hesitation. It's not a clean break like a bone. It's not a sudden catastrophe like a fire or flood. It's a slow unraveling, a quiet bleeding out, a wound that won't close.

In these chapters, I'll take you through two loves that changed me and two losses that nearly broke me. Chelsea, whose vibrant spirit taught me to see sunset as a two-minute miracle; and Madison, my daughter, who taught me that a father's heart can keep beating even when half of it is missing.

These stories aren't just about heartache. They're about the lessons that only love and loss can teach: that presence matters more than provision. That words spoken in anger can't be unspoken. That some silences last for years. And that despite it all, love never really leaves—it just changes form.

As you read, you might recognize your own reflection in these stories. Perhaps you've also felt the ache of a phone that doesn't ring or the space left behind by someone who chose to go. Perhaps you too have learned that loving someone doesn't guarantee you get to keep them.

If so, I invite you to walk alongside me through these memories—not to wallow in sorrow, but to find, as I did, that even our deepest losses can lead us toward mercy.

5
LOVE, LAUGHTER, AND THE NIGHT SHE LEFT

Chelsea had vibrant blue eyes that seemed to laugh before her mouth did. She was the kind of woman who never met a stranger. Her smile was wide and inviting, her personality alive in every room she walked into.

We first met at a Chris Knight concert at River Road Ice House just outside New Braunfels, Texas. River Road was legendary in the Hill Country—a rustic venue with twinkle lights strung across outdoor seating areas, the smell of barbecue in the air, and the Guadalupe River flowing nearby. I had invited her, expecting a night of shared music and conversation.

To my surprise, she showed up with another guy. I hadn't expected her to bring someone else along, but I rolled with it. We still enjoyed the concert together, bonding over the music and the atmosphere. I watched her sing along to the songs, completely present in the moment, genuinely happy to be there.

That first night didn't end in romance, but it set the stage for everything that came next.

Not long after, she turned the tables and invited me on a fishing trip. She mentioned we'd be joining her mom and stepdad, so I knew this was both an outing and an introduction to her family. The day was relaxed and sunny as we cast our lines. By the end of the trip, I had filled my stinger and helped her catch one little fish, which I took home.

That evening she texted me: "Why'd you steal my fish?"

I laughed and wrote back that I didn't think anyone would want that little thing. She shot back, "Well now you owe me dinner."

That playful exchange set our first real one-on-one date in motion.

Later that week, we met at my condo. I cooked the fish with her by my side, the kitchen filled with the sound of sizzling butter and the smell of seasoning. When everything was nearly ready, we paused for a moment, standing eye to eye in the warm light. Inches apart. My heart pounded. I leaned in and kissed her.

It was gentle and unexpected, but it felt completely natural. We both smiled, a little surprised at how fast the spark had grown. Dinner could wait. We kissed again, a little longer this time. The room felt like it was spinning and steady all at once.

Afterward, we sat down to our modest meal and laughed about how it was more symbolic than filling. Then we carried a couple of beers outside and talked under a star-studded Texas sky, peeling back layers we hadn't yet shared.

In the weeks that followed, a little tradition emerged for us. A small bar-and-grill down at the marina became our spot. Nachos piled high, two cold beers, and sunsets over calm water. Sometimes we'd talk about everything, sometimes nothing at all.

One evening, as the sun lowered toward the tree line, I told her something I'd noticed: "Once the sun hits the tree line, it's completely gone in about three minutes."

She laughed, pulled out her phone, and timed it. That night, the sun disappeared in two minutes and forty-seven seconds.

It was a small moment, but it stuck with me. Time feels longer than it really is. Three minutes can vanish in the blink of an eye, or it can hold a memory you'll carry for a lifetime. Since then, I've tried to treat sunsets like those two minutes and forty-seven seconds—something to stop for, to savor, to respect.

I can still see her in those golden hours—leaning on the table, smiling as the breeze caught her hair, last light reflecting in her eyes. The nachos and the beer weren't the point. It was about presence, about spending those fleeting minutes together.

She balanced me. I was wound tight, always calculating the next step, the next responsibility. She was light and easy, always reminding me that life wasn't just about surviving.

One night, she decided to make me a steak sandwich. Her food was always incredible—she could make magic out of random anything in the fridge. I sat there, watching her cook, when the knife slipped. She sliced her hand wide open, blood running down, but she laughed it off.

"Still finishing your sandwich," she joked. That was Chelsea—giving, even when it cost her something.

Random nights with her turned into adventures. Once, we ended up at Tejas Rodeo. We had a few beers, watched riders get thrown into the dirt, and danced under the string lights. Later, wandering through a pasture, we spotted a house lit up in the distance.

"Looks like a party," she said with that mischievous grin. "We should crash it."

Before I could even respond, she was halfway across the field, dragging me along. That's when we noticed the bull.

He was massive, freshly ridden, and not in the mood for visitors. His eyes locked on us. Chelsea gasped, but I puffed up, trying to be her protector.

"We're fine," I said. "I grew up working dairy farms."

Then the bull stood up and started walking toward us. My bravado cracked. He picked up speed, and suddenly we were sprinting for the cattle guard. A car slowed nearby—for a moment we thought they'd help—but then they sped off, leaving us in the dirt.

I looked over, and Chelsea was already gone, running like lightning. The bull thundered closer. I ran harder than I ever had, lungs burning, until I hit the cattle guard and collapsed. She laughed, brushing dirt off her jeans.

"Didn't have to be faster than him," she teased, "just faster than you!"

We laughed until our sides hurt. That was us—chaos turned into memory.

We weren't always laughing, though. Chelsea struggled with depression. I knew it, but I didn't always know how to handle it. She wanted my presence. Just me beside her. But I drowned myself in work, chasing security, convincing myself that providing was the same as loving.

After a year together, we found our "forever home"—a beautiful lake house where you could see the sun rise over the lake, planning futures in each corner. But things weren't as perfect as the photographs we hung on the walls. I slept downstairs more often, claiming it was so my early mornings wouldn't wake her. The truth was more complicated.

Unresolved resentments were rising between us, creating an invisible wall even as we shared the same address. But there was something else I didn't fully understand yet—the frontal lobe damage from the motorcycle wreck was still doing its silent work. Impulse control, emotional regulation, the ability to step back before reacting—these were compromised in ways I hadn't addressed. I thought I'd healed because my bones had mended and the scars had faded. I hadn't done the deeper work, the cognitive therapy that might have given me tools to manage what was happening inside my head. That reckoning would come later, forced by what followed. I just wish I'd gotten there sooner.

When I was furloughed from the rigs, she told me she'd fallen for the peaceful guy who spent every day trout fishing. "That was the man I wanted," she said. "But when you went back to work, the weight came back. And you hid it until it consumed you."

She was right. I was scared all the time. After I got laid off, the money drained fast. I obsessed over building something—hustling, grinding, desperate to prove I could make it work. She would have ridden it out with me, through anything, if I had just let her in. But I didn't.

Then came the night.

We had driven to Medicine Park, not for a creek-side dinner but to climb. The old town sits at the base of Wichita Mountains, its cobblestone streets leading up to vistas where you can watch the sun set over Oklahoma. Chelsea wanted to catch that sunset, so we hiked to a rocky outcropping as the light turned gold.

I have a photo from that moment: her hands raised and curved into a heart, the orange sun burning through the space between her fingers. It still feels like a postcard from a life that might have been.

After the sun dipped below the peaks, we headed toward Lawton for a couple of beers. What should have been an easy night turned heavy. Sitting at the bar, we both felt the weight of bills and time apart; unspoken resentments filled the empty space between us. Chelsea stared at the condensation on her glass and asked, quietly, why we kept missing each other.

I had no answer that didn't sound like an excuse.

The drive back to the vacation rental I'd just purchased was silent except for the hum of the road. The house was supposed to be a symbol of stability—the start of a foundation so I could escape oilfield rotations. Instead, it became a battleground.

As soon as we walked inside, Chelsea said she was going to sleep in the spare bedroom. It wasn't said with anger; it was a weary sigh, a request for space.

I could have let her have it. I could have offered to talk the next morning when we were both rested.

Instead, I followed her.

I didn't knock. I stepped into that room ready to win an argument rather than save a relationship. The words I chose were not truth; they were weapons. I dredged up her depression and twisted it into a blade. I threw her insecurities back at her as if hurting her would somehow prove I still mattered.

When I finished, I stormed off and slept on a couch in another room, convinced that the silence would force her to chase me. She didn't.

By morning, her bag was packed. Keys on the counter. No note. Gone.

In the days that followed, I called and texted until my fingers hurt. When she did answer—weeks later, to collect the rest of her things—she listened to my apologies without expression.

"I believe you're sorry," she said at last. "I just don't believe anything will change."

She closed the door, and with it the chapter of us.

Later, I tried to apologize to her mom. I loved her too—she had become family. She reminded me gently that Chelsea wasn't always easy either, trying to soften my guilt. But soon after, her cancer returned.

When she passed, I went to the funeral. People stared when I walked in. I could feel the uncertainty—why was I there? I signed the register, sat in the back, and stayed quiet. Chelsea and I made eye contact once, brief and loaded. We both knew the reason I came. It wasn't my place to make grief heavier than it already was.

I left by the side door.

It was the last chance I had to say goodbye, and I said it in silence.

What hurts now isn't just losing Chelsea. It's knowing that on a mountaintop, with her hands framing the sun, I had a chance to choose presence over pride. The mercy I talk about later in this book had not yet taken root in me. In that cabin bedroom, anger still ruled. I didn't need to be right. I needed to be kind.

I learned that too late for us, but the lesson would shape every step that followed.

REFLECTION: Love and Loss

Losing Chelsea wasn't just losing a partner. It was losing balance, humor, and the reminder to play.

The night she left taught me that presence matters more than provision, and silence is better than words sharpened to wound.

I will always carry regret for the words I chose, but I will also always carry gratitude for the time I had with her.

➤ Think of a time when you hurt someone by what you said. Or think of a time when someone you loved left you. How did you feel afterward? How did you change as a person?

MERCY PRACTICE: The Sleep Rule

When emotions run hot and words threaten to turn into weapons, try implementing this practice:

1. Establish the Sleep Rule with important people in your life: No major relationship discussions after 9 p.m. or when either person is tired, hungry, or stressed.

2. If a difficult conversation starts to escalate, raise your hand in a gesture to stop both of you. When you calm down enough, say, "I care about this conversation too much to have it when neither of us is at our best. Can we pause and pick this up tomorrow morning?"
3. Write down what you want to say and let it sit overnight instead of saying it in the moment. This creates distance between the emotion and the expression.
4. When you resume the conversation, begin with, "I want to understand your perspective better" before stating your own.

This practice isn't about avoiding hard conversations. It's about having them when both people can bring their best selves, not their sharpest weapons. The most important discussions deserve our clearest minds. Take it from me. I learned the hardest way.

Losing Chelsea broke something in me. But as painful as that loss was, nothing could prepare me for what came next: watching my daughter—the center of my world—slowly drift away until one day, she asked me to sign myself away.

6
SANTA HUNTS AND SILENT GOODBYES

Madison was fearless from the start. I bought her a trail-a-bike—a little single-wheel attachment behind my adult bike meant for sidewalks, something safe for kids. But Madison wasn't satisfied with sidewalks. She insisted we take it off the sidewalk almost immediately. Before long she was bouncing behind me down mountain bike trails, laughing with each jolt. She trusted me completely. Her tiny hands gripped the bars, her little legs pedaled like she was conquering the world.

Her balance was perfect, her instinct for leaning into turns uncanny for a child her age. While other parents worried about skinned knees, Madison and I were flying over tree roots and around berms, her squeals of delight filling the forest air.

"Faster, Daddy! Faster!" she'd shout, utterly fearless, completely trusting that I'd keep her safe. And I did. On those trails, I was hyperaware of every potential danger, adjusting our line to avoid the worst drops, calling out warnings when we approached technical sections. I was more careful with her on the back of that bike than I'd ever been while riding alone.

Those days on the trails were some of my happiest as a father. I felt capable, connected, trusted. The problems that plagued me elsewhere—money, work stress, relationship tensions—they all fell away when it was just Madison and me, conquering trails together.

Christmas became our favorite time of year. I made sure of it. Driving through neighborhoods lit up with decorations, I would slam on the brakes suddenly, pointing to the sky.

"Did you see him?" I'd whisper. "Santa just flew over!"

Her eyes would widen, her whole body buzzing with excitement, as we leapt from the truck to chase shadows across lawns, running together as if we might actually catch him.

On one Christmas Eve, after she'd gone to bed, I spent hours setting up an elaborate scene. I had bought special chalk that would wash off easily and wrote a message from Santa on the living-room wall: "SANTA WUZ HERE." I scattered "reindeer food" (oats mixed with glitter) on the front lawn. The next morning, her face when she saw the evidence of Santa's visit was everything. Pure wonder. Pure magic. Pure belief. She touched the chalk letters with tiny fingers, her eyes so wide I thought they might never close again. "He was HERE, Daddy! In OUR house!"

Her belief filled the room. Another year, I stayed up until 3 a.m. rigging fishing line from the living-room ceiling fan to make small stuffed animals "fly" in circles. When she woke up and saw them spinning slowly in the morning light, she gasped, convinced Santa's magic had brought her toys to life.

Every December became a performance of joy, a game, a chance to let her live in the magic as long as possible.

I realize now I wasn't just trying to make Christmas magical for her. I was trying to prove to myself that I could create wonder even when everything else felt like it was falling apart.

And it wasn't just holidays. I gave her every vacation day I had. Trips to the Alamo and other landmarks became history lessons. She soaked it all in. Her teachers noticed, and once they even let her teach the class when the subject came up. She spoke with confidence because she wasn't just repeating facts from a book. She had been there. She had lived it.

That night, she called me from her mom's house, bursting with excitement. "Dad! Guess what! My teacher let me tell the class about the Alamo today!" Pride swelled in her voice as she recounted how she'd stood at the front of the room, explaining the history, the significance, and the details she remembered from when we'd stood together at those old stone walls. Afterward her teacher pulled her aside to say how impressed she was. Pride surged through me—not just because Madison was smart, but because something I had done as a father had given her this confidence, this knowledge.

Those were the highs. The moments that felt like fatherhood at its best. But the lows cut deeper than I thought possible.

The french fries story was the beginning of it. The moment in the truck when I couldn't even buy her a small bag. That moment cracked me open because it wasn't about food—it was about my failure to provide, to protect, to be enough.

And the cracks widened as she got older. When the oilfield took me away for weeks at a time, I told myself I was providing.

That was love, wasn't it? But distance creates silence, and silence grows into space you can't always cross.

While I was off working rotations, Madison's world kept spinning without me. I missed her gymnastics. Missed school plays. Wasn't there to answer questions about homework. I did send money. I did call when I could. But I wasn't there, not in the ways that mattered most.

I remember once, after a brutal rotation—fourteen days of twelve-hour shifts in scorching heat—I flew in specifically to see her. A friend lent me his house so we could have some time together. I was so exhausted that I fell asleep on the couch almost immediately. When I woke up, she was gone.

She had called her mom, scared. She said she didn't know where she was supposed to sleep.

I would have given her my pillow. My blanket. The floor itself if it meant she felt safe. But even when I made a special effort to be there, I was too exhausted to be there in the way she needed me to be, and the silence between us only grew.

Her birthdays became markers of the growing distance. At ten, she still ran to hug me when I showed up. At twelve, she offered a stilted hello. By fourteen, my calls went straight to voicemail.

Then came the moment that gutted me. Madison, my little girl, asked me to sign away my parental rights.

There are no words for how it feels to hear that. It wasn't a question. It was a request loaded with the weight of everything I had done wrong—every absence, every missed moment, every scar I had left without meaning to.

What do you do when the person you love most says they want to cut the tie between you?

I was faced with an impossible choice. If I fought it, she might feel I was ignoring her needs, clinging to my rights over her happiness. If I signed, I risked losing her forever—but maybe, maybe she'd come back one day knowing I hadn't forced her. I signed. And five years later, I'm still waiting in silence.

The Thanksgivings and Christmases are the hardest. Once, she had been the center of my holiday traditions. Now, I spend those days alone, often by the lake, remembering how it felt to have her little hand in mine as we chased Santa through strangers' yards.

One Thanksgiving, I sat by myself on a dock, eating a sandwich, watching families set up picnics nearby. A raccoon—I named him Randy—crept closer and closer, eyeing my food. I tossed him bits of bread, laughing at his careful approach, the way he'd wash each morsel in the water before eating it.

"It's just you and me, Randy," I said aloud. "Happy Thanksgiving."

He cocked his head, as if considering my words, then scurried off with his prize. Even the raccoon had somewhere better to be.

I've tried many ways to bridge the silence. I created a blog called "Messages to Madison"—a collection of life lessons, stories, and advice I wanted to share with her. I knew she might never read it, but I needed to put the words somewhere, to send them out into the world as if they might somehow find her.

In one post I wrote, "Anger makes a terrible compass. It will always point you toward destruction, never toward peace. When you're angry, wait. When you want to lash out, breathe. The words you don't say in anger are never regretted."

In another: "The hardest people to love are often the ones who need it most. This includes yourself."

The blog became my way of parenting from a distance, of offering guidance without intrusion, of loving without demanding love in return.

If she called tonight—right now—I know exactly what I would say. Not, "Where have you been?" or, "Why haven't you called?" but simply, "Are you okay? How have you been? What choices did I make that led us here?" And then I would listen, without defense, without justification, for as long as she needed to speak.

I keep one seat open at my table. Not a shrine, not a place setting with her name, just an empty chair. It's a reminder that there's always space for her return, for difficult conversations, for starting over if she ever wants to.

We've all experienced the pain of watching someone we love pull away. Whether it's a child, a parent, a friend, or a partner, slow distancing hurts in a way physical pain never could. The hardest part isn't the separation itself—it's the wondering. Did I try hard enough? Could I have done something differently? Will they ever come back?

These questions have no easy answers. But I've learned that the space between people isn't always permanent. Sometimes it's a necessary chapter in a longer story. Sometimes the distance itself is what allows healing to begin.

REFLECTION: Love That Never Leaves

Some losses don't scar over. Some wounds stay open, raw and aching, no matter how much time passes.

Love sometimes means letting go, even when every part of you wants to cling tighter. Signing those papers didn't mean I stopped being her dad. It meant I was willing to bear the pain of absence if it gave her peace.

The silence hurts. It always will. But my love hasn't gone quiet. It waits, like the memory of Santa in the sky, ready to come running if she ever calls.

➤ Think of a person you loved or cared for who pulled away from you and exited your life. How have you processed the grief? What have you learned?

MERCY PRACTICE: One-Text Repair

When someone you love feels distant, try this practice instead of overwhelming them with contact or withdrawing completely:

1. Write a simple text message that:
    - Acknowledges their perspective ("I understand you need space").
    - Takes responsibility without conditions ("I'm sorry for what I said").
    - Offers connection without pressure ("I'm here if and when you're ready").

2. Before sending, ask yourself, "Is this about their needs or mine?" If it's about making you feel better, rewrite it.
3. Send only ONE message, then respect their silence. Repeated attempts at contact often push people further away.
4. Set a specific time period (like a month or six months) before reaching out again, and honor that timeline.

This practice teaches patience and respect for others' boundaries while keeping the door open for reconnection. The most meaningful repairs often begin with a single, honest message followed by the space to respond in their own time.

Losing Madison was the deepest wound. But in the silence that followed, I discovered that salvation sometimes comes on four legs, with a wagging tail and an unwavering presence that asks nothing but to be near you. WEEK TWO OF THE 30-DAY CLIMB

If you've completed Week One of the Climb, you've already proven something important: You can show up twice a week, even when it's hard. Now we build on that foundation by adding one more intentional day.

Week Two asks for three intentional days. Just three. Not seven, not five—three. This gradual progression is deliberate. It allows your body and mind to adjust without the shock that leads to resistance and abandonment.

The four anchors remain the same:

- MOVEMENT: Do something physical.
- REFLECTION: Write one page in your journal.
- CONNECTION: Reach out to someone.
- MERCY: Give yourself grace at least once.

But in Week Two, I want you to add one small challenge: On at least one of your intentional days, push a little further in one of these areas. For example:

- If your movement has been walking, try adding a short jog.
- If your reflection has been surface-level, explore a painful memory.
- If your connection has been text messages, make a phone call.
- If your mercy has been general, pinpoint a specific failure to forgive.

This slight increase in intensity builds resilience without triggering the all-or-nothing mindset that derails so many attempts at change.

Here's what a Week Two tracker might look like:

WEEKTWOTRACKER

Days committed: three.

DAY 1: ________ (date)

[ ] MOVEMENT: What I did: ________.

[ ] REFLECTION: One page written.

[ ] CONNECTION: Whom I reached out to: ________.

[ ] MERCY: Where I extended myself grace: ________.

DAY 2: ________ (date)

[ ] MOVEMENT: What I did: ________.

[ ] REFLECTION: One page written.

[ ] CONNECTION: Whom I reached out to: ________.

[ ] MERCY: Where I extended myself grace: ________.

DAY 3: ________ (date)

[ ] MOVEMENT: What I did: ________.

[ ] REFLECTION: One page written.

[ ] CONNECTION: Whom I reached out to: ________.

[ ] MERCY: Where I extended myself grace: ________.

My ONE small push this week was: ________.

Notes:

____

____

____

And here's a sample journal entry from my own Week Two experience:

SAMPLE JOURNAL ENTRY – DAYTWO-WEEKTWO

I pushed myself in the Connection category today. Instead of just texting Tommy, I called him. The conversation wasn't long—maybe ten minutes—but it was real.

He asked about work. I almost gave my usual "fine, busy" answer, but something stopped me. Instead, I told him the truth—that I've been feeling hollow lately, going through the motions without purpose.

His response surprised me. "Join the club," he said. "Everyone feels that way sometimes. The difference is whether you keep showing up anyway."

It wasn't sympathy. It wasn't advice. It was solidarity. And somehow, that helped more than a thousand "it'll get betters" ever could.

I realized something after the call: Connection isn't about performance. It's not about having good news to share or solutions to offer. It's about being honest about where you are and letting someone else be honest too. It's about saying "me too" instead of "you should."

Tomorrow might be harder. I might slide back into hollow automatic responses. But today, for ten minutes, I was real with someone. And that counts.

As you navigate Week Two, remember:

- Your three days don't have to be consecutive.
- Quality matters more than duration.
- Progress isn't linear—some days will feel like steps backward.
- One small push is enough to build momentum.

You're building more than habits here. You're building identity. Each time you follow through on a commitment, you're telling yourself a new story: "I am someone who shows up. I am someone who tries. I am someone who keeps climbing, even when the trail gets steep."

Madison's absence left a hole in my heart that nothing could fill. But in the darkest moments after she left, when I questioned whether life was worth continuing at all, an unexpected companion arrived. A small Australian Shepherd puppy with mismatched eyes who would quite literally save my life.

PART THREE

STRENGTH AND BROTHERHOOD

When your own strength fails, sometimes the only thing that keeps you standing is someone else's belief in you. In the darkest periods of my life—when I couldn't see a way forward, when the voice in my head said "quit"—it was the steady presence of others that became my foundation.

The chapters ahead introduce the companions and mentors who lent me strength when mine had run out: Nodens, the Australian Shepherd who saved my life through simple, unfailing loyalty; Jono, the former Ranger who refused to let me quit on a mountain climb, teaching me that the body gives up long before the will does; and the giants who showed me what real strength looks like—not the ability to never fall, but the courage to get back up again and again.

These aren't stories of lone heroism. They're stories of interdependence, of the power that comes when one person says to another, "I see you struggling, and I'm not going anywhere." They're reminders that we were never meant to climb alone, that the strongest among us are those who know when to reach for a helping hand.

As you read, I invite you to consider the companions in your own life—the ones who saw you at your worst and stayed anyway. The ones who believed in you when you couldn't believe in yourself. The ones who showed you what strength really means.

Because the truth I've learned is this: The company you keep will either lift you up or pull you down. Choose wisely. And when you find those rare souls who make you better by their presence, hold on tight. They are the brotherhood that will help you conquer mountains.

7
THE DOG WHO SAVED ME

When I first saw Nodens, he was just a tiny ball of fur, small enough to fit in my hands. The breeder opened the pen and out tumbled a blur of paws and ears. But he didn't hesitate—he came straight for me, as if he knew I was his before I did.

I wasn't looking for a dog that day. I wasn't looking for anything except maybe a way to avoid standing in line alone. Life had become a series of losses, one after another, until I started to wonder if there was any point in continuing. The pain had become a constant companion, more familiar than happiness, more reliable than hope.

But when faced with yet another long wait for something mundane and forgettable, I made a different choice. "Might as well go look at puppies." It wasn't about getting a dog. It was about avoiding the emptiness of standing still with my thoughts.

The breeder's place was nothing special—a simple stall for working on equipment, a coffee trailer where I would get my caramel macchiato with three extra shots and protein powder every morning, and a fenced area where the puppies played. Australian Shepherds, she told us. Smart, loyal, high-energy. I nodded, not really listening.

Then the gate opened, and this one puppy—with one blue eye and one brown—made a beeline for me. He climbed onto my boots, looked up at me with those mismatched eyes, and something in my chest shifted.

"That one likes you," the breeder said.

I picked him up, and he immediately nuzzled into my neck, his tiny body warm against my skin. For the first time in months, I felt something other than numbness or pain. I felt . . . chosen.

At the time, I was barely hanging on. Life felt like a string stretched too tight, ready to snap. But I couldn't take him home yet—he was too young, only a few weeks old. So for the next four weeks, I visited him every day. Sometimes I'd just sit with the breeder, watching him tumble around with his littermates. I'd bring approved treats, hold him, let him fall asleep in my lap.

Those visits became ritual. No matter what else was falling apart in my life, no matter how dark the day, I showed up for that puppy. It gave me a reason to get out of bed, leave the houseboat where I was now living, and drive somewhere with purpose.

Those visits became the only consistent thing in my life—the one appointment I wouldn't miss, the one promise I kept no matter how dark the day. When everything else felt pointless, this small commitment anchored me: Be there for Nodens. Show up. Don't let him down.

When he finally came home with me, I scraped together what little money I had to send him to board-and-train to become a certified service animal. I worked with a psychiatrist to have him prescribed as a service animal. His job was simple on paper:

to calm the handler during episodes. In reality, he had the hardest job in the world—keeping me alive when I didn't always want to be. While he was in training, I was deployed in the field for work, checking in with the trainers whenever I could get signal, counting down the days until we'd be together again.

When I finally brought him home to the boat, he adapted as if he'd been born for it. I was living mostly on the water then, renting out my house as a vacation property just to make ends meet. Nodens learned the boat fast, padding confidently along the docks, tail wagging as if this was the life he had chosen.

His favorite treat was a Pup Cup. The first time he tasted whipped cream from the little cup, his eyes widened with joy. From then on, every time I said the words "Pup Cup," he'd run to the door, tail wagging, sitting patiently until we left. At the coffee shop, he knew exactly what was coming. He'd wait in line with me, eyes locked on the counter, patient but buzzing inside. And when he got it, he'd lick the cup clean, whipped cream covering his nose. It was ridiculous. It was perfect.

Our days fell into a rhythm. Morning walks along the shore, where he'd chase birds but never catch them. Afternoons on the boat, him sprawled in a patch of sun while I worked on repairs or paperwork. Evenings at the local dog-friendly bar, where he'd become something of a celebrity, greeted by name while I remained "Nodens' dad" to most.

He had this uncanny ability to sense my moods. On the darkest nights, when sleep wouldn't come and thoughts spiraled toward the abyss, he'd press his body against mine with an almost human understanding. His weight became an anchor, his steady breathing a metronome that my own would eventually match.

One night, when the darkness was heavier than usual, I sat on the edge of the dock, staring into the black water below. Thoughts of simply slipping in, of letting the weight in my chest pull me down, were louder than they'd ever been. Nodens, sensing something was wrong, wedged himself between me and the water's edge. When I tried to move him, he planted his feet, refusing to budge. He wasn't aggressive—he was insistent. His eyes locked with mine, and the message was clear: Not tonight. Not while I'm here.

I broke down then, sobbing into his fur, clutching him like a lifeline. He stayed perfectly still, absorbing both my weight and my grief, until the storm passed. Only then did he lead me back to the boat, never leaving my side until morning.

But the oilfield called me back, and the job wasn't a place for a dog. At first, I begged friends for help. I wore out every favor, leaving Nodens with whoever would say yes. Eventually, one friend stepped up and took him in regularly. We joked about "shared custody." It wasn't ideal, but at least I knew he was safe.

On Father's Day—a particularly painful holiday given my situation with Madison—I came home from rotation to find Nodens had chewed up my newest boat project, a *Sidebar*, an addition that meant a lot to me. hoses were scattered across the floor and destroyed.

For a split second, anger flared. I raised my voice, and Nodens immediately dropped to the ground, ears flat, eyes wide with fear. The sight stopped me cold. This wasn't just normal dog submission—this was terror. He thought I would hurt him.

In that moment, I made him a promise I've kept ever since: "I will never make you look like that again." I got down on the floor with him, speaking softly until he crawled toward me, still wary. It took almost an hour of gentle reassurance before he fully relaxed.

That day taught me something crucial about how damage travels—how my own unhealed wounds could become the source of someone else's fear. Nodens was just a dog being a dog. The problem was my reaction, my inability to manage my emotions in the face of a minor loss.

Training Nodens became a form of training myself. The techniques I learned—clear communication, consistent boundaries, patience through setbacks—applied as much to my own growth as to his. His e-collar corrections happened outside, but the verbal commands had to match inside the house and everywhere else. Consistency mattered. I couldn't be one person in public and another in private. He needed to trust that I was the same man, everywhere, always.

We developed rituals together. Sunday mornings were for the barber—me for a haircut, him for a nail trim at the groomer next door. The first time I dropped him off, he pouted, genuinely offended that I would leave him with strangers. When I picked him up, his entire body wiggled with joy, forgiveness immediate and complete.

That was a lesson too—how quickly he moved past disappointment, how ready he was to celebrate reunion rather than punish separation. Dogs don't hold grudges. They don't weaponize silence. They live fully in each moment, a skill I was desperately trying to learn.

Then came Rio.

A friend was rehoming a Frenchie, and I thought maybe it would help. French Bulldogs had been part of my life before, back when Chelsea and I got our first pair. I convinced myself Rio would balance things out.

But Rio had other plans.

Cute as could be but a little jerk, Rio decided quickly that he was mine—and that Nodens needed to step aside. He'd shove his way between us, hogging attention, claiming space that Nodens had earned.

At first, it hurt me to see Nodens pushed out of the spotlight. But Nodens never flinched. He stayed calm. He waited. He remained loyal, watching me with those steady eyes that seemed to say, "I'm not going anywhere."

That's when I realized that he was teaching me adaptation. Love isn't always about having the spotlight. Sometimes it's about waiting, steady and patient, knowing where you belong no matter who else comes and goes.

The most remarkable thing about Nodens wasn't any trick or skill I taught him. It was his intuition—his ability to sense my mental state even before I fully registered it myself. On mornings when depression pressed heavy, before I'd even opened my eyes, he would be there, nose pressed to my face, refusing to leave until I got up. On days when anxiety spiraled, he would place himself firmly against my legs, a living reminder to stay grounded.

He seemed to sense the moments when my thoughts turned dangerous. There were nights—more than I care to admit—when the idea of ending things felt like the only escape from pain. On those nights, he would refuse to leave my side. He would wedge himself between me and the door, or simply place his weight across my chest, his eyes never leaving mine.

Once around 4 a.m. I was pacing on the dock, my mind racing with failures and regrets. Nodens shadowed me step for step, a quiet guardian. As dawn broke, casting pink light across the water, I finally sat down, exhausted. He climbed into my lap—all forty-five pounds of him—and rested his head on my shoulder. We stayed that way until sunrise fully bloomed, neither of us moving, just breathing together.

In those moments, I understood what was happening: This wasn't just a dog comforting his owner. This was one soul recognizing another in pain, and refusing to let it suffer alone.

Nodens saved me. Not with heroics, not with loud declarations, but with quiet presence. With loyalty that never wavered. With love that never left.

We often talk about rescuing animals, about giving them homes and second chances. But sometimes it's the animals who rescue us. They don't judge our failures or keep score of our mistakes. They don't hold our past against us or demand we become something we're not. They simply stay, witnessing our lives in all their messy imperfection, loving us not despite our flaws but with a completeness that includes them.

We've all experienced the healing power of unconditional love—whether from a pet, a friend, or a stranger who showed kindness when we least expected it. That kind of love doesn't ask us to be fixed before we're worthy of connection. It meets us exactly where we are, in all our brokenness, and says, "You are enough, right now, just as you are."

REFLECTION: Loyalty That Heals

People may leave. Some by choice. Some by silence. Some by circumstances too heavy to control. But loyalty can heal in ways nothing else can.

And sometimes, when we're lucky, it shows up with four paws, mismatched eyes, and the uncanny ability to know exactly when we need to be saved from ourselves. Nodens reminded me that love doesn't have to be loud. Real love simply stays.

➢Have you ever been deeply comforted by a dog or cat or other pet? What was it that comforted you? How was it similar to or different from my experience?

MERCY PRACTICE: Animal Connection Breathing

When anxiety, depression, or racing thoughts take over, try this practice with a pet if you have one or with someone else's pet if it works:

1. Sit or lie down with your pet close enough to touch.
2. Place one hand gently on your pet, feeling their warmth and the rhythm of their breathing.
3. Begin to synchronize your breath with theirs. Animals naturally breathe more slowly and fully than humans do when we're anxious.

4. Count four breaths together. Notice how your pet stays present in the moment, not worried about yesterday or tomorrow.
5. Say aloud, "Thank you for being here with me right now."

This practice grounds you in the present moment through physical connection with a being that lives naturally in the now. Even without a pet, you can practice by imagining this connection or by observing wildlife outdoors.

Nodens taught me that sometimes the strongest companions aren't the ones who push you to your limits but the ones who simply refuse to let you face the darkness alone. But there were other kinds of strength I needed to learn—the kind that comes from brothers who see your breaking point and say, "Not today. Not on my watch."

8
TOUGH BROTHERHOOD

Jono was a Ranger—the kind of guy who carried himself as if every challenge was just another day at the office. He ran something called Hairy Scary Evolutions, pushing people through brutal training sessions designed to break you down and build you back stronger. He showed up at races, always cheering, always making you feel ten feet tall.

I met him through Matt, the owner of the gym where I trained. Matt knew I was struggling. He particularly knew I needed something to push me beyond the walls I'd built around myself. "There's someone you need to meet," he said one day, and introduced me to Jono at the gym. Jono didn't talk much about his time in the Rangers. He didn't need to. It was evident in everything about him—the way he assessed situations, the economy of his movements, and the depth in his eyes that spoke of things seen and unseen.

He had a way of looking at you that cut through the crap. When Jono said, "You've got this," you believed him, even if your body was screaming otherwise.

After my accident, when my body still remembered pain more than performance, Jono convinced me to ride the Six Gaps in North Georgia. Six mountain passes, one after another, totaling more than a hundred miles and nearly 11,000 feet of climbing. Even for able-bodied riders, it was infamous.

I had no business being out there. My body was broken, and my head was not far behind. But Jono believed in me—and sometimes, that's enough to make you try.

The morning of the ride dawned clear and cool, a deceptively beautiful day for what was coming. We gathered at the starting point, bikes gleaming, muscles warm from stretching. Jono gave a brief overview of the route, pointing out the steepest climbs, the technical descents, and the spots where we could refuel.

"Remember," he said, looking each of us in the eye, "your body will give up long before your mind does. When your legs say stop, your heart says slow, and your head says quit—that's when the real ride begins."

I nodded, trying to believe it. Looking at the other riders—lean, strong, confident—I felt like an impostor. My knee still had broken cartilage floating around. My joints still ached with every move. But Jono had said I could do this, so I clipped in and followed the group out.

The first climb shredded my lungs. My legs screamed, my chest burned, and my heart hammered as if it were trying to break free of my ribcage. Riders passed me, some with nods of encouragement, some with pity in their eyes.

By the second gap, I was furious—at the road, at my body, and at life. Every pedal stroke was a negotiation with pain. Every breath was a battle. I started talking to myself, first under my breath, then out loud, a stream of profanity and determination that probably frightened anyone who passed too close.

When I hit the descent, my hands trembled on the bars, white-knuckled, every bump rattling through my frame. The speed should have been exhilarating, but all I felt was fear—fear of crashing again, fear of more broken bones, fear of failure.

The third gap broke me physically, but I kept going. The fourth broke me mentally.

Halfway through the fourth climb, I snapped.

I hurled my bike off to the side of the road and collapsed into the grass. Sweat poured, my vision blurred, and I yelled into the trees, "I'm done! I can't do this!"

Jono pulled up beside me, calm as ever. "Get up." "Fuck you," I spat back. "Get the car. I'm finished."

He didn't move. He didn't lecture. He just looked at me with those steady Ranger eyes. The kind that had seen worse than this. The kind that said quitting was never the end of the story.

"There's no car coming," he said finally. "You either ride out or you sit here all day."

I swore more, creative combinations that would have made a sailor plug his ears. Jono simply waited, straddling his bike, and took a drink from his water bottle.

"You can be pissed," he said. "You can hurt. You can cry if you need to. But you're getting back on that bike."

It wasn't a request. It wasn't even a command. It was a statement of fact, as certain as gravity.

Eventually, I dragged myself back onto the bike. I made it a little farther before collapsing again. Three of the six gaps. Half the ride. Half the mountain. Half the proof I wanted to give myself.

When I couldn't go any farther, Jono didn't berate me. He didn't tell me I'd failed or come up short. He simply said, "You showed up. You pushed until you couldn't push anymore. That's the win today."

I didn't conquer Six Gaps that day. But Jono never let me call it a failure.

To this day, he talks about me as if I can do anything. Not because I crushed the ride, but because I showed up broken and still gave what I had.

That's the thing about brotherhood—especially among vets. We see each other's cracks. We don't hide from them. And when one of us wants to quit, the other just stands there, steady, reminding us of who we really are.

Jono taught me that failure isn't in falling short of a goal. It's in not showing up. It's in letting fear keep you on the couch instead of on the road. It's in believing the voices that say, "You can't," before you've even tried.

Scott Rigsby was a different kind of inspiration altogether. I met Scott during my recovery from the motorcycle accident, when I was clawing my way back into the world. We shared a coach and endured the same brutal Wednesday night spin classes—two and a half hours long, designed to break you.

Scott was a double amputee, training for the Ironman. He hadn't crossed that finish line yet, but he trained as if his life depended on it. Sweat pouring, eyes locked, legs pumping on prosthetics as if they were built from steel and not plastic.

I had been told I might never run again. Watching Scott grind, I realized that excuses had no place in the room. Pain wasn't the end. It was the beginning of a different kind of strength.

Scott had a saying that stuck with me: "Small adjustments early beat heroics late." He was talking about race nutrition and pacing, but it applied to everything. Make small corrections now—in your training, your recovery, your
life—and you avoid the need for desperate measures later.

I would watch him make tiny adjustments to his prosthetics during training, a quarter turn here, a slight shift there. Nothing dramatic, just consistent fine-tuning. And I realized that's how you come back from devastation—not in one heroic leap, but in a thousand small adjustments, day after day.

When he finally did cross that Ironman finish line, it wasn't just his victory. It was proof to everyone who had ever been told they couldn't—that they could.

Then there was Tommy. A retired Air Force major. He was the kind of man whose words carried precision, weight, and always, always accuracy.

I met Tommy during a pivotal transition in my life. I'd just moved to San Antonio, trying to rebuild after a series of setbacks. Tommy owned several rental properties and had a room available. But this was no ordinary landlord-tenant relationship.

The first time I saw his kitchen, I knew I was dealing with someone different. Every shelf was labeled. Every container was organized. It wasn't just tidiness—it was a system, a manifestation of a mind that valued order and clarity above all.

Tommy became more than a landlord. He became a mentor, a partner, and eventually a father figure.

Once we sat at a table with others, and someone asked him if he believed in aliens. Without hesitation he said, "They're real," and began laying out his reasoning. I stopped listening. It didn't matter what the explanation was. If Tommy said they were real, then they were. His word carried that much weight with me.

Another time he used the word *intrinsic*. I had to look it up later. But that was Tommy. Always digging deeper, always seeking what was at the core. That word stuck with me. Intrinsic value. It became a pillar for how I measure things even today.

When I had nowhere to go after one of life's many disasters, Tommy didn't just offer a roof. He offered a model. Clean kitchen. Labeled shelves. Systems over guesses. He showed me how to create order from chaos, not just in a living space but also in decision-making.

One day we were dealing with a tenant who regularly violated noise rules despite multiple warnings. I was frustrated, ready to confront the situation with the same anger that had solved nothing so far. Tommy pulled me aside and simply said, "Make a fucking decision."

It wasn't about the tenant. It was about me, about the pattern of avoiding clear boundaries and then exploding when they were crossed. Tommy was teaching me that leadership—of others or of self—requires decisions, not reactions.

That lesson led to us eventually co-owning properties together. We would sit at his kitchen table, reviewing numbers with brutal honesty. No inflated projections, no wishful thinking. Just the cold, hard truth of what was and what could reasonably be.

Once we walked away from a deal that on paper looked incredible. Yet the numbers were lying—barely, but enough that Tommy spotted it. Months later, that property became a money pit for whoever bought it. Tommy's insistence on truth over optimism had saved us the equivalent of a college tuition.

Tommy showed me that leadership wasn't about barking orders. It was about presence. About being calm when others broke. About knowing your values so deeply that people trusted you without question.

These men—Jono, Scott, and Tommy—were brothers to me in the truest sense. We did not share blood, but we shared values, battles, and growth. They saw in me what I couldn't yet see in myself. They held me accountable without holding my past against me. They showed me what strength really looks like—not an absence of weakness, but a willingness to move forward despite it.

We've all had moments when we wanted to throw the bike off the road and quit. When the mountain seemed too steep, the journey too painful, the goal too far away. In those moments, what often makes the difference isn't our own resolve, but the presence of someone who refuses to let us surrender to our smaller selves.

Whether it's a training partner who shows up at your door on days you'd rather stay in bed, a mentor who holds you to a higher standard than you'd hold yourself, or a friend who simply says, "I believe in you" when you've lost all belief—these connections form the backbone of resilience.

REFLECTION: The Company You Keep

The company you keep decides whether you stay broken or begin to heal.

Jono taught me that sometimes you don't need someone to carry you. You just need someone who refuses to let you quit. Someone who stands in the road, looks you in the eye, and says without words: You're capable of more than you believe.

Scott showed me that excuses dissolve in the presence of someone overcoming obstacles far greater than my own.

And Tommy demonstrated that true strength isn't emotional or physical. It's the clarity to see reality as it is, make decisions based on truth rather than wishful thinking, and move forward with precision.

Choose your company wisely. Seek out those who make you stronger by their very presence. Be that person for others when you can. Because in the end, we climb together or we fall alone.

➤Do you have, or have you had, anyone in your life who is like a brother or sister that does not let you wallow or hold back, but encourages or pushes you in ways you need? What did that person do? How did it make a difference in your life?

MERCY PRACTICE: Lifters List

When you feel stuck or defeated, try this practice to reconnect with the strength others see in you:

1. Create two columns on a page: "Who Lifts Me" and "How They Lift."
2. In the first column, list three-to-five people who make you better, stronger, or more hopeful by their presence.
3. In the second column, write specifically what each person brings out in you. Not what they do for you, but who you become by being around them.
4. Choose one person from your list and reach out with a specific message: "When I'm around you, I feel more [quality they bring out]. Thank you for that gift."
5. Finally, ask yourself, "Who might include me on their Lifters List?" And, "How can I be that kind of presence for someone else today?"

This practice reminds you that strength is often relational—found not just within yourself, but in the connections that bring out your best qualities. By acknowledging these relationships, you activate their power even when the person isn't physically present.

Jono, Scott, and Tommy were my immediate brotherhood—men whose daily presence shaped who I was becoming. But there were also others whose impact, though more distant, was no less profound. Giants whose stories and examples stood as lighthouses when my own path seemed darkest.

9
GIANTS WHO MADE ME STAND

As with the three brother figures, I had still others help me walk this road. Every time I thought I had nothing left, someone appeared and showed me a mirror—not of who I was, but of who I could be. Giants. Men who carried scars of their own, who made me realize survival wasn't about being unbroken. It was about standing up anyway.

David Goggins—thepush-upgauntlet. Everyone who knows David Goggins has a story. Mine starts in the Air Force, when my buddy Troy Hamman and I went to his house for a workout.

We expected a list of exercises, something insane and structured. Instead, he looked at us with that flat, unblinking Goggins stare and said, "The push-up."

I frowned. "Okay. . . . And what else?"

"The push-up," he repeated. "Each of us will do 500. And the next man doesn't start until you finish."

I thought he was joking. Sixty push-ups in, my arms shook. Seventy-five, I collapsed. Goggins wasn't phased. He picked me up by the shirt, dropped me back down, and barked, "Keep going."

There was no encouragement in his voice. No rah-rah motivation. Just the cold expectation that I would continue, regardless of what my body thought was possible.

By the time we staggered out of that workout, our arms useless, I couldn't even lift a coffee cup the next morning. My elbows locked from lactic acid, and my muscles were shredded. The battalion NCO had to release me to sick call for ibuprofen and muscle relaxers.

We still laugh about it today. But it wasn't just a workout. It was a lesson in mental toughness. Goggins embodied the truth that the body gives up long before the mind does. He showed me that my limits weren't where I thought they were.

Years later, I would read Goggins' book and recognize in those pages the same man who had pushed me past collapse that day. His philosophy—that most of us tap into only a fraction of our potential, that comfort is the enemy of greatness, that growth happens when we deliberately seek out suffering—had been demonstrated to me in person, through hundreds of push-ups I thought I couldn't do.

The lesson wasn't about physical capacity. It was debunking the stories we tell ourselves about what we can and cannot endure. Goggins' gift to me was showing me those stories were largely fiction.

Scott Rigsby—training with fire in his eyes. I met Rigsby after my motorcycle accident, when I was clawing my way back into the world. We shared a coach and endured the same brutal

Wednesday night spin classes—two and a half hours long, designed to break you.

Rigsby was a double amputee, training for the Ironman. He hadn't crossed that finish line yet, but he trained like his life depended on it. Sweat pouring, eyes locked, legs pumping on prosthetics as if they were built from steel and not plastic.

I had been told I might never run again. Watching Rigsby grind, I realized excuses had no place in the room. Pain wasn't the end. It was the beginning of a different kind of strength.

What impressed me most about Rigsby wasn't just his physical perseverance, though that was remarkable. It was his clarity of purpose. He wasn't just training for himself. He was training to prove something to the world, to show what was possible for amputees, to change perceptions and open doors.

He would talk about this sometimes during breaks in training, voice low but intense. "It's never just about the finish line," he'd say. "It's about who's watching you get there."

That perspective transformed how I viewed my own struggle. I wasn't just healing for myself. I was showing others what recovery could look like, what resilience meant in practice, not theory.

When he finally did cross that Ironman finish line, it wasn't just his victory. It was proof to everyone who had ever been told they couldn't—that they could.

Jim MacLaren—a spark from a distance. I first learned MacLaren's story while sitting at a computer, barely surviving my own rehab. Oprah was on in the background, and there he was—a man who had lost his leg in a motorcycle accident, then been hit again and paralyzed from the chest down. His tragedy became the spark that inspired the creation of the Challenged Athletes Foundation.

His words hit me like a freight train. Here I was, wallowing, and this man had found purpose in devastation.

Unlike Goggins and Rigsby, I never met MacLaren in person. But his story reached me at exactly the right moment, when I needed to see that hardship could become meaning, that suffering could transform into service.

I reached out and eventually connected with his brother and sister. We spoke, and through them, I felt as if I knew him. He has since passed, but his story never left me. Even now, I stay in contact with his family. His life and his courage lives as a spark in me.

What MacLaren taught me—from a distance, through others' telling of his story—was that our worst moments can become our greatest contributions. That the deepest pain, when transformed, can lead to the most significant impact.

Tommy—the steady voice. If I had to distill Tommy's impact into a single lesson, it would be this: Integrity isn't a lofty ideal—it's practical. It's making decisions based on truth rather than convenience. It's speaking with precision rather than exaggeration. It's acting consistently with your stated values, even when no one is watching.

These men—Goggins, Scott, Jim, Tommy—they were giants. Not because they were unbroken, but because they refused to stay down. They stood, and by standing, they made me stand too.

We all need giants in our lives—those rare individuals whose examples shine so brightly it illuminates our own path. They may not be famous. They may not have platforms or audiences. But through how they live, they show us what's possible when courage meets circumstance.

Think of your own giants. The teacher who saw potential in you that you couldn't see yourself. The friend who demonstrated loyalty when everyone else walked away. The parent or grandparent whose quiet strength became the foundation of your own. The stranger whose kindness in a dark moment reminded you of humanity's capacity for good.

These are the shoulders we stand on. These are the examples that pull us forward when our own strength fails. These are the giants who make us stand.

REFLECTION: Standing on Shoulders

We don't survive on willpower alone. We survive because someone, at some point, looks at us and says, "You can."

Sometimes their voice is loud, like Goggins dragging you off the floor. Sometimes it's quiet, like Tommy reminding you that values matter. Sometimes it's watching from a distance, like Scott grinding through pain, or Jim turning tragedy into purpose.

These men stood tall, and when I leaned on their shoulders, I found I could stand too.

➤Do you have, or have you had, people in your life or personalities you've admired who have inspired you to go beyond your self-imposed limits? What was it they did? How has that changed you?

MERCY PRACTICE: Giants Gratitude

When you need strength beyond your own, try this practice to connect with the giants in your life:

1. Identify one person who has shown you what's possible through their own example. This could be someone you know personally or someone whose story has impacted you from afar.
2. Write down three specific qualities they embody that you admire. Be concrete: not just "strength" but "the ability to speak truth even when it costs them."
3. Reflect on one time when thinking of this person helped you make a better choice or persevere through difficulty.
4. If possible, reach out to express gratitude. Be specific about how their example has influenced you. If they're no longer living or accessible, write the letter anyway. The act of articulating it matters.
5. Finally, identify one quality of theirs that you can embody today, in some small way. How can you stand a little taller on their shoulders?

This practice reminds us that strength is often transmitted through example. By consciously connecting with our giants, we activate their wisdom and courage in our own lives.

WEEKTHREEOF THE 30-DAY CLIMB

If you've made it through Weeks One and Two of the Climb, you're already building momentum. Two intentional days became three. Small pushes expanded your comfort zone. Now we take another step forward: four intentional days.

Why four? Because it represents the tipping point. When you commit to four days a week of intentional practice, you're showing up more days than not. The scales begin to shift. What once felt like effort starts to feel like identity.

But remember—this isn't about perfection. It's about progression. About proving to yourself, one day at a time, that you can trust your own word.

The four anchors remain your foundation:

- MOVEMENT: Do something physical.
- REFLECTION: Write one page in your journal.
- CONNECTION: Reach out to someone.
- MERCY: Give yourself grace at least once.

In Week Three, I encourage you to focus on depth in one area. If movement has been your strongest practice, explore a new type of challenge. If reflection has been surface-level, dive deeper into uncomfortable truths. If connection has been digital, make it face-to-face. If mercy has been general, make it specific to a particular wound.

Here's what a Week Three tracker might look like:

WEEKTHREETRACKER

Days committed: four

DAY 1: ________ (date)

[ ] MOVEMENT: What I did: ________.

[ ] REFLECTION: One page written.

[ ] CONNECTION: Whom I reached out to: ________.

[ ] MERCY: Where I extended myself grace: ________.

DAY 2: ________ (date)

[ ] MOVEMENT: What I did: ________.

[ ] REFLECTION: One page written.

[ ] CONNECTION: Whom I reached out to: ________.

[ ] MERCY: Where I extended myself grace: ________.

DAY 3: ________ (date)

[ ] MOVEMENT: What I did: ________.

[ ] REFLECTION: One page written.

[ ] CONNECTION: Whom I reached out to: ________.

[ ] MERCY: Where I extended myself grace: ________.

DAY 4: ________ (date)

[ ] MOVEMENT: What I did: ________.

[ ] REFLECTION: One page written.

[ ] CONNECTION: Whom I reached out to: ________.

[ ] MERCY: Where I extended myself grace: ________.

My focus area this week was: ________.

What I noticed about going deeper in this area: ________.

Notes:

____

____

____

____

____

____

____

____

____

____

____

And here's a sample journal entry from my own Week Three experience:

I went deeper in the reflection category today. Instead of just writing about what happened or how I felt, I forced myself to look at a pattern that keeps showing up: my need to be right more than my need to be connected.

It happened again yesterday with Mark. We disagreed about a project timeline, and I went straight to proving my point instead of listening to his concerns. I "won" the argument, but the tension between us is still there. Was being right worth the distance it created?

This pattern goes back as far as I can remember. With Chelsea, with Madison, with coworkers. I'd rather be right than vulnerable. I'd rather win the point than strengthen the relationship.

I wonder where I learned this. Maybe from my father, who never admitted he was wrong. Maybe from the military, where being wrong could have consequences. Maybe it's just fear—if I'm not right, then who am I?

The cost is getting too high. I'm tired of creating distance to protect my ego. I'm tired of being "right" and alone.

Tomorrow I will call Mark. Not to rehash the argument, but to ask what he was actually worried about beneath the timeline issue. And I will listen—really listen—without planning my response while he talks.

Being right might feel good for a moment. Being connected feels good for a lifetime.

As you navigate Week Four, remember:

- Four days is challenging but achievable.
- Depth matters as much as frequency.
- Track patterns and insights, not just completions.
- Celebrate progress without demanding perfection.

You're halfway through the 30-Day Climb. The trail is getting steeper, but your legs are getting stronger. The view from here already shows how far you've come. Keep climbing.

The brothers and giants who surrounded me provided external strength when my own reserves ran dry. But eventually I had to face an uncomfortable truth: All the physical endurance and warrior mentality in the world couldn't heal the deepest wounds.

10
TOO BROKEN TO QUIT

March 20, 2004. Three months before the accident. The day I learned that sometimes you continue not from strength, but because stopping requires more energy than continuing.

I stood at the starting line and felt out of place immediately. The other runners looked like they'd stepped out of an ultra running magazine—lean, calm, stripped down to almost nothing. At most, someone had a small water bottle, and even that was empty. They talked strategy, pacing, which climbs to respect and which to push. I had no strategy. No pacing plan. My only plan was the most primitive one I could think of: one foot in front of the other until either I collapsed or I crossed the line.

On my back was a Camelback stuffed with 100 ounces of flat Coke mixed with carb powder and another 100 ounces of water. I'd packed like I was headed into combat: energy gels, bars, extra socks, even a roll of 100mph tape in case an ankle rolled or a blister started burning. It felt smart in my kitchen, but standing there next to men and women carrying nothing but a half empty bottle, it already felt like a mistake. The straps dug into my shoulders before the gun even fired. I didn't say it out loud, but in my head I was already afraid the weight on my back would be the reason I didn't finish.

Madison was only nine months old. Too little to remember anything, of course, but she'd been there for it—watching, in her own way, as I pieced myself back together after the accident. Your mother was supportive—she always was when it came to these races, as long as we could afford it. When Vern Winter, one of my favorite fitness clients, told me about Oak Mountain, she didn't even blink. "Only $35? Go for it."Vern had said, "You should run the Oak Mountain 50K! It's not far and it's cheap!"

I'd never heard of ultra marathons. The furthest I'd ever run was ten miles, and that was a military formation run□ —□ not by choice. But it was months away when I registered. Plenty of time to train.

Except I didn't. Nine months flew by. This was Madison's first time at one of my events. Work consumed everything. I ran exactly five miles once in those four months.

Standing at that start line, friends who saw me tried to talk me out of it. "You only ran five miles in four months?"

"I want my race shirt," I said.

"You can still get the shirt without running."

"If I don't complete a race, I can't wear the shirt."

That's when I made myself a promise: when that gun goes off, I'm starting this race. I will only accept crossing the finish line or complete failure and life flight. No other options.

The gun went off. The race started across about three hundred yards of open field before the course funneled into the tree line. By the time my shoes hit the dirt, my heart rate was already redlined. My lungs burned like I'd been sprinting instead of jogging into the woods. That's when the truth hit me: no training, no base, no business being here. My first thought was blunt—oh shit, this is going to be a really long day. Every step into those trees, doubt poured in. I questioned my prep, my judgment, even whether I'd make it past the first climb. I wanted to believe I could grit it out, but right then, all I felt was panic.

The course wound more than thirty-one miles of single-track, climbing and dropping over thirty-six hundred feet with no mercy. On paper it sounded like adventure—Double Oak Mountain twice, Pea vine Falls near the ridge, Maggie's Glen shaded and serene. In reality, it was pure punishment. The climbs stripped every ounce of energy, leaving my legs shaky and my lungs clawing for air. The downhill's weren't relief; they were torture. My quads screamed, my knees buckled, every step felt like it might finish me. The metal in my rebuilt body protested with each impact.

The roots and rocks turned the trail into a minefield—catch one with a tired foot and my whole body would lock in spasm, the threat of a twisted ankle or blown knee hanging over every mile. And then the creeks—cold shocks to an overheated body, jolting me awake for just long enough to remember how much more I had left to go. It felt endless.

March in Alabama decided to set records. Eighty-six degrees. At one checkpoint, no water they'd run out. I met three seasoned ultra runners who all agreed this was the hardest ultra they'd ever done. Between the heat, the elevation, and my spectacularly bad preparation, misery had found me and was picking away at my brain.

Mile twenty-six was the decision point—the last sag stop with vehicles, the last real chance to step off the course. My body was wrecked. Every step sent pain shooting through me, every muscle past the point of begging. I wanted to quit so badly it almost hurt worse than the running. I stood there consuming whatever calories I could hold down, shoving food and drink into a stomach that barely cooperated, arguing with myself in circles.

The volunteers explained: "Several miles, all downhill from here. But the checkpoint or the finish are the only two ways out."

I really wasn't sure I was capable. I knew I didn't want to walk back uphill to leave. *Wait, it's all downhill from here? How bad can that be? Plus, Ryan, remember what you told yourself?*

Finally, impulse won. Go.

I dropped downhill a hundred yards before the thought crashed over me: *No, I'm done. I can't do this.* I turned back, ready to surrender—but to quit meant climbing back uphill to the sag stop. My body refused. I didn't have the strength to walk back out.

So I went on. Another hundred yards, another wave of doubt. I knew I couldn't make it. Turned again—same wall, same impossible climb back. I stood there breathing hard, heart hammering, realizing I was trapped by my own exhaustion. Either I died on that trail or I finished. Those were the only options left. I took a deep breath, braced myself, and let gravity carry me further down the mountain.

What I didn't know about mountain running: long descents destroy you in ways climbs don't. Your quads work overtime to brake. Your knees take the impact. Every step is controlled falling. A quarter mile in, I realized this. Maybe it was time to wise up and throw in the towel. I turned and looked back at that climb. My body refused to go up. The only way out was through.

Somewhere in the trees I started to hear it—the muffled sound of voices, the finish line calling through the woods. It hit me like a surge of electricity: I was actually going to make it. After everything, after every step I thought would be my last, I was going to cross that line.

I tried to pull it together for those watching. Coming around the restrooms, I saw them—my stepson Alex, my exwife, and Madison. Nine months old, too young to know the significance or even the experience. The finish line. The cutoff clock showing 8:50.

I straightened myself as best I could, put on my best game face, and tried to summon a run for the last hundred yards. My version of a run looked more like a hobble, but I forced it anyway.

Eight hours and fifty minutes. Ten minutes before cutoff. Out of seventy-two finishers, I was number sixty-eight. Sixty-eighth out of seventy-two, sixtieth out of sixty-two men. Many didn't finish. By any measure, unimpressive.

But to me, it was everything.

Even when finishing is the only option left.

The ride home, fever of 101.9, throwing up any food I tried to eat, everything hurt. I made it home and barely managed to get to my Sunday morning shift.

There was no money won. No fame. My body took serious damage. But the personal lessons from that day have carried through every aspect of my life since:

- Even with all odds against you, that doesn't mean you can't.
- Heart and the right mindset can make or break you.
- When commitment to yourself becomes a core value, it becomes extremely powerful.
- The noise in your head lies to you.
- Every thought pushing you toward quitting is fear based.
- Don't be scared to set goals beyond what you think you're capable of.

The reality was simple: most considered my finish impossible. Hell, so did I. But that was the moment I realized something that would stay with me forever—if I was willing to fully commit, to silence the chatter between my ears, I was capable of far more than I had ever imagined.

Think of a time when you wanted to give up but discovered that quitting would have required more energy than taking one more step forward. What did that moment reveal about your resilience?

MERCY PRACTICE: The Too Broken to Quit Rule

- When exhaustion and self-doubt urge you to stop, pause and mentally turn around. Ask yourself: What does quitting actually require? Does walking back demand more effort than moving ahead?

- If going backward means climbing out of a hard place, let gravity and momentum carry you forward. Sometimes the easiest path is the one right in front of you.
- Recognize that being too tired to quit isn't weakness—it's physics. Use that truth. When willpower fades, let the simple act of putting one foot in front of the other pull you toward the finish.

11
THE TURNING POINT

It didn't happen all at once, but rather in small moments of clarity that built up over time. I remember standing in the quiet after yet another sleepless night, realizing for the first time that my stubborn endurance had become a cage. The strength I once prized was now keeping me from the healing I desperately needed.

Pain has a way of convincing us that we must outlast it, that simply surviving makes us victorious. But there comes a time when the cost of holding on outweighs the fear of letting go. My turning point was not a dramatic revelation—it was a slow surrender to the truth that I could not do it all alone.

I began to seek out moments of stillness, to notice what surfaced when I stopped pushing so hard. Sometimes, what surfaced was grief, regret, or worry. Other times, unexpected hope crept in. Each time I allowed myself to listen, I moved one step closer to the help I needed, and further away from the self-imposed isolation of the warrior's mindset.

The hardest battles, I realized, are the ones fought inside ourselves. And sometimes the bravest act is to put the armor down, invite vulnerability in, and trust that healing can begin in the quiet aftermath. For the first time, I was ready to find out what might grow in that space.

For that, I needed a different approach—one that began not with fighting harder, but with laying down arms altogether.

PART FOUR

HEALING AND PRACTICE

There comes a point in every journey when you realize that what got you *here* won't get you *there*. For me, that moment came after years of powering through—surviving floods and fires, pushing my broken body past its limits, grinding through work rotations and relationship failures with the same white-knuckled determination.

I had survived. But I wasn't living. And I wasn't healing.

The chapters ahead mark a turning point—from warrior to student, from fighting to flowing, from judgment to understanding. They tell the story of what happened when I finally admitted I couldn't power through the deepest wounds, when I sought help, when I learned that true strength often looks like surrender.

You'll meet David, the therapist who taught me to retire the warrior without losing the strength. You'll witness what happened when I applied that learning in the oilfield, where calm meant survival and explosive leadership cost lives. You'll see how flow replaced fight, how empathy expanded my world, and how I discovered that the only real apology is change.

These aren't stories of overnight transformation. They're accounts of stumbling practice, of two steps forward and one step back, of gradually building a different kind of muscle memory. They're reminders that healing isn't an event—it's a daily commitment to showing up differently, even when old patterns feel safer.

As you read, I invite you to consider your own patterns. The ways you've learned to survive might now be keeping you from thriving. The armor that once protected you might now be weighing you down. These can turn into battles you keep fighting long after the war has ended.

Because the truth I've learned is this: Sometimes the bravest thing you can do is lay down your weapons, open your hands, and allow mercy to flow—first to yourself, then to others.

12
RETIRING THE WARRIOR

"The warrior isn't dead. He's alive in you. But his fight is done."

David, my therapist, leaned forward in his chair, his eyes steady on mine. It was our fifth session, and he had just dropped a bomb on everything I thought I knew about strength.

I hadn't wanted to be there. Therapy wasn't part of my vocabulary. Where I came from, where I'd served, you handled your problems. You pushed through. You didn't talk about feelings to a stranger in a quiet office with plants and calming music.

But I was bleeding out slowly. Not physically—that kind of injury I understood. This was different. I was losing myself, one relationship at a time, one outburst at a time, one night too many of staring at the ceiling and wondering if there was any point in continuing.

Choosing help wasn't a moment of clarity. It was desperation. It was knowing that if I didn't change now, there wouldn't be anything left to change later.

The first sessions were awkward. I gave short answers. I deflected with humor. I talked about events but avoided emotions. David never pushed. He just created space, waited, and occasionally asked a question that cut through my defenses as if they weren't even there.

"What would it cost you to be wrong?" he once asked after I'd described an argument with a coworker.

"What do you mean?"

"If you admitted you were wrong in that moment, what would that mean about you?"

The question landed like a gut punch. I had no answer.

"It would mean I'm not . . . reliable," I said finally. "That my judgment can't be trusted."

David nodded. "And in your world, in the environments where you've survived, what happens to people who can't be trusted?"

The answer was immediate: "They get left behind."

And there it was. My need to be right, to never show uncertainty, to power through even when I was clearly wrong—it wasn't arrogance. It was survival. It was fear of abandonment so deep I'd buried it under layers of stubbornness and certainty.

That revelation was just the beginning. Over weeks and months, David helped me understand how much of my identity had been shaped by the warrior archetype. The fighter. The one who never quits, never shows weakness, never needs help. It had served me well in many contexts—military service, the oilfield, and physical recovery from injuries. But it was destroying my capacity for connection, for vulnerability, and for peace.

"The warrior gets you through the battlefield," David explained. "But he's a terrible companion for daily life. He sees threats everywhere. He can't rest. He can't receive. He can only fight or prepare to fight."

I thought about all the relationships I'd damaged by treating every disagreement like combat. All the moments I'd missed by being on guard instead of being present. All the help I'd rejected because accepting it felt like weakness.

"So what?" I asked. "I just kill that part of myself? Pretend I was never a warrior?"

That's when David said the words that changed everything: "The warrior isn't dead. He's alive in you. But his fight is done. You don't have to meet every hurdle ready to attack anymore. You can learn to flow."

He introduced me to meditation, but not in the way I expected. No apps, no cushions, no chanting. Just simple in-the-moment breathing. Three breaths: in for four counts, hold for four, out for six. It was a reset button for when my emotions started to spiral.

"You don't need twenty minutes of meditation," he said. "You need three breaths before you speak when you're angry. You need to recognize when the warrior is taking over and give him the ability to stand down."

The concept of retiring the warrior—not killing him, not shaming him, but thanking him for his service and letting him rest—became a powerful image for me. I could visualize it: the sword laid down, the armor removed, the constant vigilance relaxed.

This wasn't about becoming weak. It was about becoming whole and recognizing that different situations called for different aspects of myself. The warrior had his place, but so did the student, the friend, the mentor, and the listener.

David also introduced me to what he called "the Sleep Rule": no relationship discussions after 9 p.m. or when either person is tired, hungry, or stressed. It seemed almost too simple, but it addressed a pattern I'd fallen into repeatedly—letting emotions escalate at night when defenses were low, saying things I couldn't take back.

"You wouldn't make major financial decisions when you're exhausted," David pointed out. "Why would you make relationship decisions—which are arguably more important—in that state?"

Another practice we developed was scheduling tough conversations. Instead of ambushing someone with a grievance or letting it fester until it exploded, I would say, "I'd like to talk about something that's bothering me. When would be a good time in the next day or two?"

This simple shift changed everything. It gave both people time to prepare, to come to the conversation from a place of intention rather than reaction. It signaled respect. It demonstrated that the relationship mattered more than the immediate release of expressing frustration.

In one session David had me visualize my warrior self—not to banish him, but to honor him. To see him clearly, to acknowledge what he had helped me survive, to thank him for his service. Then in my mind's eye, I saw myself taking the sword from his hands, laying it on a rack, and stepping back.

"He's still there," David said. "You can call on him when you truly need him. But he doesn't need to run the show anymore."

Learning to retire the warrior wasn't a single moment of transformation. It took a daily practice of catching myself when I slipped into combat mode over minor issues. It was developing new muscle memory—breathing before speaking, choosing connection over being right, allowing silence instead of filling it with defensiveness.

There were setbacks, times when the warrior took over before I realized what was happening and times when old patterns felt safer than new uncertainties. But slowly, session by session, practice by practice, something shifted. Not just in how I acted, but in how I saw myself and the world.

We all carry parts of ourselves that once helped us survive but now limit our ability to thrive. For some it's the perfectionist who protected them from criticism but now prevents joy. For others it's the people-pleaser who kept them safe from conflict but now erases their own needs. For me it was the warrior—always alert, always ready for battle, always certain.

Recognizing these patterns is the first step. Honoring them for how they served us is the second. And gradually, thoughtfully learning to loosen their grip on our lives is the work of true transformation.

REFLECTION: Retiring the Warrior

The parts of yourself that helped you survive may be the very parts now keeping you from living fully. This isn't about self-rejection. It's about integration—understanding when certain aspects of yourself are helpful and when they're harmful.

For me, retiring the warrior meant learning that not every disagreement is a battle, not every emotion is a weakness, and not every request for help is a surrender. It meant discovering that there is strength in vulnerability, power in pause, and wisdom in uncertainty.

This isn't about becoming soft. It's about becoming whole.

➤If you look at your life, your history, you will almost certainly see behaviors or mindsets that once helped you cope or survive or overcome, but they have since become hindrances and problems in themselves. What are those in your life? How do you respond to recognizing them?

MERCY PRACTICE: The Three-Breath Reset

When emotions threaten to overtake you, try this practice:

1. Recognize the trigger. Notice when your body tenses, your voice changes, or your thoughts accelerate. These are signs that your reactive self is taking control.
2. Three breaths: Inhale for four counts, hold for four counts, exhale for six counts. Repeat three times.
3. During the third exhale, silently say to yourself: "Not every battle is mine."
4. Only then, speak or act.

This practice creates space between stimulus and response. It gives you time to choose your reaction rather than being driven by it. Use it before difficult conversations, when feeling overwhelmed, or anytime you notice your warrior self-preparing for unnecessary battle.

Retiring the warrior in the therapist's office was one thing. Putting it into practice in the real world—especially in environments where warrior energy was the currency of respect—would be another challenge entirely. The oilfield would become my testing ground, where I would learn whether calm could replace combat in the most demanding circumstances.

13
SANDPAPER TO THE SOUL

The oilfield is unforgiving. It doesn't care who you are, where you came from, or what you've survived. It chews through men and spits them out, leaving scars on the ones who last. The roar of 90–100 db diesel engines fills the air as we push fluid down hole, the relentless noise a constant reminder of the power and danger that surround us. The heat, the dust, the grime—they cling to every surface, every pore, every breath. When I first started, a supervisor named OT leaned in close and offered advice that would become a creed: "No matter what happens, stay calm. If there's fear in your voice, if there's panic in your eyes, everyone else will follow it. If you stay steady, they'll steady too."

Calm in chaos. Years later, I was a supervisor running a frac job. The bleed-off manifold sat seventy-five feet in front of me when a 2 inch plug valve bonnet gave way at 11,000 PSI. A hundred-foot wall of high-pressure water shot into the Texas sky. You couldn't hear it over the pumps, but you couldn't miss what it meant. Chaos erupted, but OT's words came back. My voice went over the radio—calm, urgent, steady: "Shut down the pumps. Bleed off pressure. Secure the area." I knew the situation had the potential to escalate quickly, so I focused on giving each person clear, simple tasks. By leaving nothing to chance and directing everyone's efforts, we managed the crisis in a timely manner, preventing further damage or injury. Afterward, the company man chuckled. "Damn, you're a fracking son of a bitch!" I grinned. Calm isn't the absence of fear; it's refusing to let fear become contagious.

Not every leader was like OT. One supervisor made it his mission to break me down. "You're a retarded piece of shit," he'd bark, loud enough for everyone to hear. His constant belittling and harassment created a toxic work environment, sapping morale and productivity. The crew and I coped by turning his abuse into a running joke. We'd sarcastically refer to ourselves as "the lazy, retarded pieces of shit," using humor to rob his words of their power. When he was eventually removed, the change was immediate. The crew's attitude improved, and their effort increased. It was a stark reminder of the impact a leader's behavior can have on a team.

Sandpaper rotations. The grind made everything worse. Hundred-hour weeks blurred into months. Burnout wasn't a possibility; it was guaranteed. When I was home, I hid in projects—Harleys, trucks, boats—anything to avoid facing the demons inside. It felt like sandpaper against the soul. Each day rubbed me rawer. But like sandpaper, it was doing something else: polishing me. Underneath the rawness, a new kind of resilience was forming.

A lesson in respect. Before I became a supervisor I was the senior operator on a new crew. Ricky, the crew's supervisor, called me in before we ever set foot on location. "Do you want to be a supervisor?" he asked. I'd been strung along so many times that I shrugged. "It'll happen when it's meant to." Ricky wasn't having it. "No," he said. "Is it your goal?" I nodded. "Then I'll do all I can to help you. But if I'm hard on you, it's because I see something in you. Give me your best—it helps me reach my goals too." He stuck to his word. He rode me hard, gave me no breaks, but he moved mountains to get me to supervisor school. That taught me a priceless lesson: When you identify someone's goal and commit to helping them achieve it, they'll move mountains for you in return. Leadership isn't just about giving orders; it's about aligning your ambitions with the ambitions of those you lead.

Culture shock and close quarters. My first rotation in Saudi Arabia was eye-opening. I expected living conditions similar to what I was used to, but instead, I found myself sharing a cramped room with three other men, two of us on day shift and two on night shift. Privacy was a luxury, and personal space was virtually nonexistent. The multinational workforce brought with it a range of cultural differences, some more jarring than others. Simple things like the lack of toilet paper in certain areas, served as constant reminders that I was far from the comforts and conventions of home. The isolation, coupled with the demanding work schedule, took an emotional toll, compounding the ever-present stress of the job.

The infection that almost killed me. It was during this challenging time in Saudi that I noticed what appeared to be an ingrown hair on my upper lip. I brushed it off, chalking it up to the relentless heat and dust. But as the days passed, the infection spread, crusting and oozing. A co-worker pulled me aside, his face grave. "If that gets in your blood, it'll hit your brain. You'll be dead." His words sent a chill down my spine.

At a local infirmary a doctor handed me a cream. Later I learned it was the kind you'd give a baby for diaper rash. The infection continued to grow. I was sent to Dhahran, where a doctor suggested surgery, talking about taking part of my lip.

That's when my phone rang. It was my first manager from the oilfield, the man who'd hired me. "I just got the message," he said. "Don't let them do anything. I'll have you on the first flight home in the morning." His words were a lifeline, a promise of hope amidst the fear and uncertainty.

Back in the States, an American doctor took one look at the rash cream and shook his head. "It's obvious why it's not healing," he said. I'd contracted MRSA—Methicillin-resistant Staphylococcus aurous, a potentially deadly type of staph bacteria resistant to certain antibiotics. The doctor prescribed a course of IV antibiotics, followed by oral medication. Within days, the infection began to clear. After three weeks of recovery at home, I returned to Saudi, my body healed but my mind forever changed.

Saudi taught me that the most advanced industrial operation in the world can still kill you if you don't advocate for yourself. It taught me that a tiny infection can be deadlier than an explosion. It also showed me what real leadership looks like: a manager who intervened at exactly the right moment, even though I was no longer under his direct supervision.

The power of the pause. In the oilfield we often find ourselves grappling with complex problems, trying to force a solution through sheer determination and grit. But sometimes the key to overcoming a challenge lies in taking a step back and pausing to reassess and gain a fresh perspective.

Despite our best efforts with one particularly stubborn issue we faced on a job site, the problem persisted, and frustration was mounting. In a moment of clarity, I called for a break and gathered the crew together. We took a collective breath and set aside our initial assumptions and approaches. In that pause, a new idea emerged, a simple, elegant solution that had eluded us in our single-minded focus. By taking a moment to reset, we were able to see an alternative path, one that proved far easier and more effective than our previous attempts.

The power of the pause extends beyond problem-solving on the job site. It's a principle that has served me well in navigating difficult conversations and interactions. When faced with a challenging situation or a heated exchange, taking a brief pause before responding allows me to collect my thoughts, to choose my words with intention rather than reacting on impulse. That moment of deliberate silence can diffuse tension and create space for a more measured and productive dialogue.

REFLECTION: Sandpaper and Polish

The oilfield is sandpaper. It strips away what's unnecessary and reveals what's underneath. It wears you raw but polishes you too. The soul that survives comes out scarred, certainly, but also smoother and more resilient. It's the kind of polish only friction can create.

OT taught me that calm is contagious. The abusive supervisor taught me that dignity matters more than dominance.

Ricky taught me that aligning your goals with your team's goals creates loyalty no amount of yelling can produce. And Saudi taught me that sometimes the smallest threats are the deadliest—and that real leadership means stepping in to save someone's life.

What difficult situations have polished you? What did the friction teach you that comfort never could?

The oilfield is sandpaper. It strips away what's unnecessary and reveals what's underneath. It wears you raw but polishes you too. It shows you exactly who you are when everything goes wrong. The soul that survives the sandpaper comes out scarred, certainly, but also smoother and more resilient. It's the kind of polish only friction can create. And sometimes, if you're lucky, someone makes a phone call at the right moment and pulls you back from the edge.

➤What difficult or challenging jobs or life situations have you been in that have taught you valuable life lessons? What were those lessons? How do you apply them to other areas of life?

MERCY PRACTICE: The Power of the Pause

Consider these lessons. Start practicing one that is most relevant to you at this time.

1. Pause before responding. When you feel triggered by an insult, a conflict, or a stressful situation, pause three seconds before speaking. This brief silence gives you control over your response rather than letting emotion dictate it.
2. Reframe insults. If someone tries to belittle you, experiment with humor or another reframe to defuse the

attack. Remember that dignity and respect bring out the best in people, including yourself.

3. Align goals with your team. Identify one person you work with and ask about their goals. Look for a way to support them. When people know you're invested in their success, they'll invest in yours.
4. Listen to your body. A small physical irritation can signal something serious. Don't ignore persistent issues. Seek proper medical advice, and don't hesitate to ask for help. It could save your life as it did mine.

Practicing these principles isn't weakness; it's mastery. It allows you to navigate the sandpaper of life without causing unnecessary friction. And sometimes that pause makes all the difference between escalation and resolution, between burnout and resilience, between rash surgery and timely antibiotics, or between breaking people down and lifting them up.

14
FLOW, NOT FIGHT

Retiring the warrior was theory; living without him was practice.

David had given me tools—breathing techniques, reframing thoughts, choosing responses instead of reactions. But tools mean nothing until you use them under pressure. Life, as always, supplied plenty of pressure.

The first real test came on a peaceful Sunday. Cresting a hill in a no-pass zone, a driver had been riding my bumper so closely I could see his face in the mirror. The irritation was already building when he decided to pass on a blind hill with double yellow lines. By the grace of God, no one was coming the other way. He put us all in mortal danger to save thirty seconds. The old Ryan would have sped up, followed him, maybe forced a confrontation—and poisoned the rest of my day.

Instead, I slowed down, moved to the shoulder, and let him go. I thought about real emergencies—valve bonnets exploding at 11,000 PSI, MRSA eating my face, Madison in my arms after the motorcycle wreck. This wasn't an emergency. It was just a man with poor judgment.

These acts of letting go were hard. Every fiber of warrior muscle memory screamed to engage, to fight, to win. But with time and effort, I engaged less in battles that didn't need my attention.

The grocery store became my meditation hall.

On a Saturday afternoon, carts bumped and children cried. Two people stood ahead of me in line. A man cut in front with an overflowing cart, pretending not to see me. Heat rose. My jaw tightened. My hands gripped the cart. Every instinct screamed to say something sharp.

Almost unconsciously, I remembered what I'd been practicing: Pause before reacting.

The line crawled. The guy behind me huffed like I owed him minutes from his life. Cart wheels squeaked. The scanner beeped. That heat climbed up my neck. So I ran David's tool, the one I could use anywhere without an app:

Inhale four. Hold two. Exhale six. Three times.

I kept my feet planted, shoulders loose, eyes down on the card reader. Three breaths took ninety seconds. The fire didn't vanish—but it moved back far enough for me to choose. The cashier slid me the receipt. I walked out with groceries—and my peace.

The Three-Breath Reset (Toolbox Format)

WHEN TO USE IT:

When your jaw tightens, your voice wants to snap, or the fire is rising—pause.

HOW TO DO IT:

1. Plant your feet. Unclench your shoulders.
2. Inhale through your nose for 4 counts.
3. Hold for 2 counts.
4. Exhale slowly through your mouth for 6 counts.
5. Repeat three times.
6. (Optional) Say to yourself: *Not every battle is mine.*

WHY IT WORKS:

Longer exhales tell your body: *we're safe now*. Your heart slows. The tension starts to break up. The breath doesn't erase your anger—but it gives you a wedge. Just enough space to choose what comes next.

Why It Matters

That breath didn't make me calm. It made me reachable. My hands loosened. My thinking returned. The moment passed—without hijacking my whole day.

I didn't win an argument. But I didn't lose myself, either. That's the shift.

Old ways of responding still cross my mind. The warrior never fully disappears—he just stops leading. I acknowledge the impulse, then let it pass like clouds.

Work provided the ultimate laboratory. After a long rotation and too little sleep, I wasn't performing at my best. Guys made jokes. The old me would have snapped back. Instead, I spoke privately with my supervisor: "I didn't bring my best today. I'll try to do better."

He shrugged. “We all have off days. Thanks for your efforts.” No drama. No need to prove anything. Just acknowledgment and moving forward. The biggest setback came when I went back to fracking.

Old habits die slow. The work tempo, crew dynamics, egos, and long hours pulled me back into old patterns. Unlike the smaller two-to-four-man crews I’d grown used to, this larger crew changed everything. At first, I found myself jumping into conversations I knew would go nowhere good. I got swept into it. But once I noticed the shift, I pulled back.

I reminded myself: words have weight. Choose them wisely.

If I sensed negativity directed at me, I engaged—fully. Thankfully this time, I was more aware. I noticed shifts in how people were reacting to me—and not in a good way. One day, it hit me: I’d rubbed everyone wrong.

I stopped. I stopped popping off. I focused on contribution—on seeing where and how I could help.

The hardest part? Accepting that I was back to being an operator. I wasn’t the supervisor here. I needed to respect the chain of command and do my job with humility. That shift—away from ego, toward contribution—changed everything.

Now, when someone asks a challenging or disagreeable question, I use the pause. With practice, it becomes normal. Just a beat of space. Enough time to stay composed and respond properly.

In all these moments, I learned something simple: the warrior had served his purpose. He kept me alive through trauma and disaster. But he didn't know how to stop fighting. Every interaction became a battle.

Flow now meant something different.

It came to mean moving like water around obstacles instead of smashing through them. It meant saving energy for fights that actually mattered, instead of burning out on every perceived threat.

REFLECTION: The Strength of Water

Consider the Grand Canyon—a monument not to force, but to patience. Water didn't blast through rock; it flowed around it. Over it. Through it. Until the rock yielded.

The warrior is dynamite—powerful, immediate, destructive. He gets results through force and fear. But he also destroys everything around the target—including the person wielding it.

Flow is water. It seems weaker at first.

The driver on the blind hill "won" if we measure by who got ahead. The man who cut in line "won" if we measure by who checked out first. My coworkers "won" if we measure by who got the last word.

But I won something more valuable—my peace.

Each breath instead of a reaction rewires the old patterns. Each pause adds strength.

This same principle applies everywhere:

– In relationships, a listening ear often shifts more than a raised voice.

– In work, steady effort beats flashes of rage.

– In growth, consistency outperforms intensity.

The grocery store isn't a battlefield. Traffic isn't combat. Work conflicts aren't wars. They're just moments. Tests of whether I've truly retired the warrior—or just buried him.

Flow chooses what's worth engaging. The warrior needs to win every battle. Flow knows most battles aren't worth fighting.

The warrior measures strength by destruction. Flow measures strength by what stays intact.

Practice It: Power of Pause & Flow (Quick Guide)

1. **Three-Second Pause**
   When you feel triggered—by a rude driver, a sharp comment, or rising heat—pause. Count to three.
   Breathe: Inhale 4. Hold 2. Exhale 6. Repeat.
   That breath slows your heart and brings your brain back online.
2. **Reframe the Moment**
   Ask: *Is this an emergency?*
   Compare it to real emergencies. Most things aren't.
3. **Choose Contribution Over Ego**
   Ask: *How can I help right now?*
   When in doubt, serve.
4. **Stay Humble**
   Letting someone go ahead doesn't mean you lost.
   It means you kept your energy for what matters.

5. **The Warrior Isn't Gone—He Just Rests**
   Strength isn't erased. It's redirected.
   Use it where it counts.

Final Thought

Practicing the pause isn't weakness. It's strength, aimed wisely.
The warrior still lives inside me. But now, he waits for the right fight.
The rest of the time—I let the water do the work. Patient. Persistent. Always finding a way through.

15
EVERYONE'S DOING THEIR BEST

I used to see the world in absolutes. Winners and losers. Strong and weak. Right and wrong.

If someone didn't meet my standard, I judged them—usually silently, sometimes out loud, and always with words sharp enough to cut. That's how I was trained. That's how I survived. Judgment felt efficient. It felt clean. It felt like control.

Pain, loss, therapy, and failure slowly stripped that lens away. What replaced it wasn't softness. It was clarity. I started to see a different truth: Everyone is doing their best.

Not their best compared to me. Not their best compared to the strongest person in the room. Their best for where they are, with what they've lived through, with the scars they carry and the weight on their back.

That shift didn't come from a book. It came from people. There was a guy who was late to crew call. Every. Single. Time.

I wanted him gone. I pushed the supervisor to cut him loose. How hard is it to show up on time? We all managed it. What was his problem?

Then we went to lunch. He told me about chronic sleep issues that turned every night into a fight. His home life was unstable. Some nights he didn't know where he'd be sleeping.

Stress and anxiety wrecked any chance of rest, and that 3 a.m. alarm felt impossible. What I had labeled as laziness was actually someone fighting just to stand up.

And my judgment was one more thing he had to fight. So I changed my approach. I already showed up early. I started knocking on his door as I walked by. "Time to get up, brother."

He started making it on time more often. More importantly, he knew someone cared whether he made it or not. I learned the same lesson from the other side. There was a time when dark thoughts wouldn't leave me alone. I reached out to someone I trusted. I didn't need fixing—I just needed to be heard. His response felt like a slap. "You don't think we all struggle with that?" he snapped.

I walked away thinking he didn't want to deal with my problems. Years later, we talked again—really talked. He admitted he'd spent most of his life wrestling with the same thoughts. He always looked successful, so I assumed he had it together. Knowing the truth gave me deeper respect for him and changed how I showed up. I stopped assuming strength meant ease. I became someone he could lean on too.

Self-judgment has been the hardest lesson of all.

I can drag myself lower than anyone else ever could. I replay failures. I stack mistakes. I sentence myself without appeal. Sometimes it takes someone else showing me compassion before I can accept that I really was doing the best I could with what I had at the time.

Those moments taught me to extend the same grace outward—and inward. On the rig, we labeled one man lazy. Slow on every task. Always finding the easiest job. Never volunteering for overtime. Easy to judge, right?

Then I learned his wife had Alzheimer's. Every night he bathed her, fed her, cared for her, and watched the woman he loved disappear one memory at a time. He showed up to work already exhausted. His "lazy" was actually him rationing the last bit of energy he had left.

Once the crew knew, something shifted. Guys picked up heavier tasks without being asked. The crew didn't get weaker—we got stronger. Because the load wasn't evenly distributed, and pretending it was had been costing us.

Lance taught me another version of the same lesson. We were both senior operators chasing the same supervisor slot. We clashed constantly—two dogs circling each other. He could've undermined me. Instead, he shared what he knew where he was strong. I did the same where I was strong.

We fought during the day and drank beers after shift. Our families met. Rivalry turned into brotherhood the moment we stopped reducing each other to competition and started seeing each other as people.

Judgment isn't limited to the oilfield. When I created the audiobook and the 30-Day Climb for my community, my intention was simple: make it free for anyone who needed it. I just hadn't had the time or bandwidth to build the platform yet.

Most people were grateful. A few accused me of profiting off pain. Those few comments cut deeper than the hundreds of quiet thank-yours. Negative words stick harder than positive ones. They echo longer. Knowing that doesn't erase the sting—but it helps me keep perspective. I refuse to let a handful of critics outweigh the many who felt seen.

The oilfield is full of broken men pretending to be whole. Divorces. Addictions. PTSD. Financial ruin. Kids who won't talk to them. Bodies held together by pills and stubbornness. We show up, do the work, and hide the rest.

But sometimes the hiding fails. Sometimes a guy is late because he didn't sleep. Sometimes he snaps because his kid is in the hospital. Sometimes he drinks too much because sobriety means feeling everything he's been running from.

And judgment zooms in on the one outburst while forgetting the hundred days he held it together.

"Seek first to understand" became my operating system. Instead of "You're always late," I try, "What's making mornings hard?" Instead of "You're not pulling your weight," I try, "This isn't like you—what's going on?" Instead of writing someone off, I try offering a lifeline.

That doesn't mean ignoring standards. Safety matters. Accountability matters. But understanding the human behind the failure changes how you address it—and whether anyone actually grows from it.

I've had people assume my intentions without ever asking. I've learned that not everyone approaches the world with curiosity. That's okay. My responsibility is how I respond.

In leadership, seeking to understand has changed everything. When someone struggles, it's easy to assume they aren't capable. More often, they haven't been trained, supported, or asked what they're carrying. When you listen first, you stop managing problems and start developing people.

Perspective-taking isn't complicated. It's stepping out of your own head long enough to imagine life from someone else's seat. It's asking, What might I be missing? It's remembering that most behavior makes sense once you understand the back story.

When I do that, I judge less. I lead better. I respond instead of react.

And when I extend that same understanding to myself, something else changes. I stop demanding perfection from a man who survived things he was never trained to survive. I stop punishing myself for choices made with limited tools. I ask a better question: Based on what I knew then, would I have done it differently?

If the answer is yes, that's growth—not guilt. Everyone is carrying weight you can't see. Everyone is fighting battles you may never know about. Everyone is doing their best—even when their best looks messy, incomplete, or disappointing.

This isn't about excuses. It's about humanity. Before you judge someone's performance, ask about their load. Before you write someone off, give them a chance to explain. Before you assume someone doesn't care, ask what's consuming their care.

That shift has changed how I work, how I lead, how I love, and how I talk to myself. Empathy isn't weakness. It's strength under control. And the more I practice it—with others and with myself—the lighter the climb becomes.

REFLECTION: The Weight We Can't See

Everyone is carrying weight you can't see. Everyone is fighting battles you may know nothing about. Everyone is doing their best with the tools they have, even when their best looks like failure. This isn't about making excuses. It's about recognizing humanity. The guy who cut you off in traffic might be rushing to the hospital. The cashier who was rude might have been screamed at by three customers before you. The coworker who snapped might be going through a divorce. We tend to fixate on negative events and comments; being aware of this bias helps us check our reactions.

"Seek first to understand" means pausing before judging, asking questions before making assumptions, listening with empathy rather than filtering everything through our own experience. I used to pride myself on being tough and having high standards. Now I pride myself on knocking on a door to help someone make it, on sharing knowledge instead of hoarding it, on seeing someone struggling and asking, "What do you need?" instead of, "What's wrong with you?" Because best is relative to capacity, and capacity varies based on what else someone is carrying. Before you judge someone's performance, ask about their load. Before you write someone off, write them a chance to explain. Before you assume someone doesn't care, ask what's consuming their care.

➤Describe a time when you prematurely judged a person for how they behaved, and then you discovered the understandable reason behind the scenes that set them up to be this way. How did you feel after the discovery? What did you learn?

MERCY PRACTICE: From Judgment to Understanding

Try the following practices. If they're too much at once, start with one and then add others as you grow.

1. Pause and ask. When you feel judgment rising, pause. Ask one open-ended question like, "What's going on in your life?" or, "How can I help?" before deciding. Practice empathic listening: Suspend your desire to respond and truly hear the answer.
2. Journal your assumptions. At the end of the day, jot down three times you assumed something about someone. For each, write what you learned after asking or observing. Over time, notice how often your assumptions miss unseen truths.
3. Acknowledge negativity bias. Recognize that negative comments or events will impact you more strongly than positive ones. To recalibrate your perspective, when criticism stings, intentionally list three pieces of positive feedback you've received.
4. Offer a lifeline. Identify one person in your life or workplace who seems to be struggling. Instead of judging, offer tangible help—a knock on the door, a ride to work, a listening ear.
5. Self-compassion check-in. Think back to a recent situation where you judged yourself harshly or felt that you fell short. Write down what happened and the self-critical

thoughts that arose. Now, imagine a close friend coming to you with the same story. What would you say to them? How would you treat them? Extend that same compassion and understanding to yourself.

6. Three-breath reset. When you feel your jaw tighten and the urge to make snap a judgment, try this:
   - Plant your feet. Unclench your shoulders.
   - Inhale through your nose for a count of four.
   - Hold for a count of four.
   - Exhale through your mouth for a count of six.
   - Repeat this cycle three times.
   - Ask yourself, "What am I not seeing here?"

That pause gives your thinking brain just enough room to return. It pulls you out of autopilot and back into choice—out of self-protection, and into connection.

Practicing these habits isn't about lowering standards; it's about raising empathy. The next time someone falls short, remember, their best may look different from yours, it may even look lousy. We're all doing our best. Even when it doesn't look like it.

So the next time you find yourself quick to judge, pause. Breathe. And ask yourself: What weight might they be carrying that I cannot see? What battle might they be fighting that I know nothing about? What if, instead of assuming the worst, I assumed they were doing their best?

That simple shift in perspective has the power to transform not only our interactions with others, but our relationship with ourselves. When we learn to extend grace and understanding outward, we create space to offer the same compassion inward. We begin to see our own struggles and shortcomings through a lens of empathy, rather than self-punishing. We start to treat ourselves as we would a beloved friend—with patience, kindness, and an unwavering belief in our capacity for growth.

Empathy isn't a weakness; it's a strength. It's the courage to sit with discomfort, to hold space for pain, to look beyond the surface and see the sacred humanity in each person we encounter. It's the key that unlocks connection, understanding, and the kind of change that lasts.

In a world that often feels divided and disconnected, empathy is the bridge. It's the way forward, the path to healing, the light in the darkness. And it starts with a simple but profound choice: to seek first to understand, even and especially when understanding is hard. Empathy chooses compassion over judgment, curiosity over assumption, and grace over condemnation.

One interaction at a time, one brave and tender act of empathy at a time, we can build a world where everyone feels seen, heard, and valued—not for who they should be, but for who they are.

And that is a world worth fighting for.

16
THE ONLY REAL APOLOGY

"I'm sorry." Two little words I've said more times than I can count. I said them to Chelsea after the words I unleashed the night she left. I whispered them to Madison in my head for years after signing away my parental rights. I muttered them to myself when I stared into the mirror at a man I didn't always recognize.

The problem is, those words alone don't carry weight. I thought if I stacked enough apologies, they might balance the scale. But apologies without action are like checks without money in the bank—they bounce.

The only real apology is change.

I had to learn that the hard way. The people I hurt—they didn't need me to keep saying sorry. They needed me to stop hurting them. They needed me to show up differently, consistently, in ways that proved I wasn't the same man who had broken them.

One of my core beliefs is that if I need to lie, then I am stepping outside of my moral compass. Honesty, especially when it's difficult, is the foundation of trust. In my professional life, this meant owning my mistakes instead of deflecting blame. It meant being transparent about my limitations and asking for help when

I needed it. With my family it meant being straightforward about my struggles and my commitment to doing better.

I've learned that any time the desire to say, "I'm sorry," arises, it's an indicator that something needs to be corrected. Rather than just offering words, I try to follow it with actions that complete the statement. If I snap at a colleague, I don't just apologize; I make a conscious effort to speak more calmly and patiently in our next interaction. If I let a friend down, I don't just express regret; I show up for them in a meaningful way to demonstrate my commitment to our relationship.

Living amends, in practice, means staying true to your virtues in the smallest of moments. The way you do one thing is how you do all things. If I compromise my integrity in a seemingly minor situation, it becomes easier to rationalize bigger transgressions. But if I practice aligning my actions with my values every day, even in the most mundane circumstances, it strengthens my ability to live with authenticity and accountability.

This isn't always easy. Changing long-standing patterns of behavior is a process filled with challenges and setbacks. When emotions flare, my first instinct is still to react the way I used to—with defensiveness, with aggression, with avoidance. The growth happens when I choose to walk away from that instinct and respond differently. It's in the pause, in the conscious choice to try a new way, even when the old way is surging.

Mercy had to start with me. For years, I carried shame like armor, convinced it was the only way to punish myself enough to change. But shame doesn't produce growth. It produces hiding. And hiding only keeps you locked in the same patterns.

Mercy isn't letting yourself off the hook. Mercy is telling yourself the truth: You failed. You caused damage. But you are not finished yet.

My therapist, David, taught me a powerful question: "Based on what I know now, would I handle things as I did then?" The answer, of course, is no. And the recognition that I would make different choices today is the first step toward self-forgiveness. It's not about excusing my past behavior, but about acknowledging my capacity for change and committing to doing better moving forward.

When I finally let mercy soften me, I stopped groveling for forgiveness and started building evidence of change. Not overnight. Not clean or perfect. But slow and steady, step by step.

Apology, I've come to understand, is not a one-time event. It's a daily practice, a continual process of aligning my actions with my values. Each morning, I set an intention for how I want to show up in the world. Each evening, I reflect on the day and write down the things I didn't get right. I commit to correcting or making amends for those missteps the following day.

Here's what I've learned the hard way: saying 'I'm sorry' means nothing if you keep doing the same thing. The words are easy. The change is hard. But the change is all that counts. Researchers have actually studied this—turns out an apology that shows you understand the hurt, paired with real action, is far more likely to rebuild trust than any words alone.

For me, this realization—that true apology lies in changed behavior—has been pivotal in my journey from warrior to healer. The warrior in me believed that strength was about never admitting fault and, never showing vulnerability. But the healer understands that real strength lies in the courage to own our mistakes, to face the parts of ourselves that cause harm, and to do the daily work of becoming someone better.

It's not a linear path. I still stumble. I still fall back into old patterns. But I'm quicker to recognize it, quicker to course-correct. I'm less focused on defending my ego and more committed to repairing the damage. I've learned that progress is not about perfection; it's about the consistency of effort, the willingness to keep showing up as the best version of myself, even when I don't get it right.

With Madison, this has meant respecting her need for distance while still making sure she knows the door is always open. It's meant writing her letters on holidays and milestone days. And it's not to solicit a response but to remind her that she is loved and thought of always. It's meant building a life of stability, sobriety, and service—a life she can step into whenever she's ready. My changing and my amends to Madison are meant to become the father she deserves, even if she never witnesses it firsthand.

In my work, living these amends has meant not only apologizing for my mistakes, but also taking tangible steps to prevent them from recurring. It's meant instituting new safety protocols after a near-miss, even when it's inconvenient. It's meant advocating for mental health resources and support for my crew, recognizing that the tough-guy culture I once perpetuated was causing harm. It's meant mentoring younger team members with patience and empathy, modeling the kind of leadership I wish I had received.

The journey of living amends is not about becoming perfect. It's about becoming intentional. It's about choosing, again and again, to align my actions with my deepest values. It's about accepting that I will make mistakes, but not letting those mistakes define me. It's about extending to myself the same compassion and forgiveness that I'm learning to offer others.

I find peace in this approach because I couldn't maintain the carnage of the direction I was heading. The weight of my regrets and the toll of my destructive patterns was unsustainable. Apology through changed behavior is not only about making things right with others; it's also about making things right with myself. It's about looking in the mirror and seeing a man I can be proud of, even with the cracks and the scars.

So to anyone I've hurt, anyone I've let down, anyone I've failed: I'm sorry. Not just in words, but in the life I'm building, the choices I'm making, the man I'm becoming. My apology is in the works, every day. And that work continues, long after the words fade.

REFLECTION: Action Over Words

Words are easy. Behavior is hard. But behavior is the only apology that counts.

It's easy to say "I'm sorry" and think the work is done. It's much harder to face the parts of yourself that caused harm and commit to changing them, day after day, choice after choice. But that's the work of a real apology.

Apology without change is manipulation. It avoids accountability while claiming remorse. True remorse doesn't just feel bad; it does better.

This is as true in the workplace as it is in personal relationships. A leader who apologizes for a mistake but keeps making the same ones isn't really sorry. A team member who says "my bad" but doesn't adjust their behavior isn't taking responsibility. An organization that issues a public apology but doesn't change its practices is performing, not transforming.

Real apology is in the quiet, unseen choices to do differently next time. It's in the humble acknowledgment that we're a work in progress, but we're committed to progress. When I choose patience over reactivity, humility over defensiveness, presence over avoidance—those are my truest expressions of remorse and repair.

I can't undo the past. None of us can. But we can all choose how we show up in the present. We can choose actions that align with our values and reflect our growth. We can choose to be the living amends for the apologies we can no longer speak.

➢Identify a way in which you made action, changed behavior, a part of your apology. What was it? What was the result? Identify an apology, or need for apology, in your life that needs to be followed by a particular action.

MERCY PRACTICE: Living Amends

Do the first item below, then the second, third, and fourth.

1. Choose one. Identify one relationship or situation where your actions didn't align with your values. Choose one specific behavior you want to change or one positive action you want to take consistently.
2. Make a plan. Break down that behavior change or action into small, manageable steps. Set a realistic timeline for implementation. Write it down.
3. Track your progress. Create a simple way to hold yourself accountable and celebrate your consistency. This could be a daily checklist, a weekly reflection, or a monthly check-in with a trusted friend.
4. Repair, don't defend. When you slip up (and you will, because you're human), focus on repairing the damage, not defending your actions. Apologize through changed behavior, not just words.

Remember, living amends aren't about perfection. They're about consistent, intentional effort. They're about aligning your actions with your values and your words with your deeds. They're about showing up as the person you want to be, even when you fall short.

Apology is a practice, not a proclamation. It's a daily choice, not a one-time event. And it's never too late to start living the apology you wish you could have made sooner. The best time to plant a tree was twenty years ago. The second best time is now. The same is true for change. Start where you are, with what you have. Start small, but start. Because the only apology that matters is the one you live.

17
BUILDING A CULTURE THAT LASTS

For years, my life was defined by chaos—reacting to whatever hit me next. Fire. Flood. Accident. Loss. Outbursts I couldn't control. I rebuilt from wreckage so many times that I started to believe life was nothing but rubble management. What I eventually learned is that stability isn't something you stumble into. It's something you build. And you build it the same way you build muscle—one repetition at a time, repeated until it sticks. Culture—whether in a crew, a family, or inside yourself—is essentially habits stacked over time. This is what some call the compounding effect: Small, consistent actions, like improving 1 percent each day, accumulate exponentially to drive significant transformation.

The gym taught me first. I'd often crash-diet or jump into a six-week beach body program only to burn out. As a trainer, I knew change doesn't happen overnight. Instead of adding more, I integrated gym time into my existing routine: two days a week, one upper body, one lower. No heroics, just showing up. After a few weeks, I wanted a third day of cardio and core. After six weeks, I looked forward to "my time." Giving up a little sleep to work out became a want, not a chore. My body followed my mind because I built the habit one session at a time.

We're beginning to understand—more clearly than ever—what happens in the brain when habits form. And it's not just willpower or repetition alone; it's a deeply physical, biological process.

Here's what's actually happening in your head when you build a habit: Every time you repeat something—same time, same place, same trigger—your brain builds a little highway. At first, you're consciously choosing. You feel the effort. You could go either way.

But keep at it, and something shifts. The choice moves deeper into your brain, into the part that runs on autopilot. What used to take willpower now just... happens.

Your brain is literally reshaping itself. The neurons involved get stronger connections. The reward chemicals start firing not just when you finish the habit, but when you see the trigger. That's why everyday cues gain so much power over us—even when we wish they didn't.

Scientists call it 'chunking'—your brain links actions into sequences you can run without thinking. That's why breaking bad habits is so damn hard. You're not just changing one decision—you're rewiring an entire routine your brain has been building for years.

The good news? Brain scans show this works both ways. Practice new behaviors with intention, and your brain physically changes. It's not magic—it's just repetition, done right.

Behavior is biology in motion. And once you understand that, you stop blaming yourself for struggling—and start working with your brain instead of against it.

The "Love Bank" came from an unexpected teaching moment with Madison. She was snarky with her friend, so I grabbed her piggy bank. "Kind deeds and nice acts are like money we put in the bank," I explained. "When life hits—a flat tire, a forgotten birthday—you to withdraw money. But you first need deposits to cover the withdrawal. If you haven't been making deposits, everything suffers." Years later, I realized I'd been teaching her what *I* needed to learn. My relationship accounts were overdrawn—too many withdrawals of anger, absence, and obsession, not enough deposits of kindness and presence. Visualizing relationships as bank accounts helped me internalize contribution. Madison understood it immediately. The metaphor gave me a simplified way to conceptualize coming from a position of contribution. It turned "be kind" into something tangible.

The Love Bank metaphor, while simple, is a powerful tool for understanding the dynamics of give-and-take in relationships. When I first introduced this concept to my daughter, it was a way to help her grasp the idea that kindness and consideration are like deposits we make into others' emotional banks. Each positive interaction, no matter how small, adds to the balance of goodwill and trust. Conversely, negative interactions or neglect are like withdrawals, depleting the emotional resources of the relationship.

This metaphor can be applied to all kinds of relationships. In romantic partnerships, consistent acts of love, support, and understanding help to build a robust Love Bank balance that can withstand the occasional conflict or misunderstanding. In friendships, being there for each other through ups and downs, celebrating successes, and providing a listening ear all contribute to a strong emotional reserve. Even in work relationships, showing appreciation, offering support, and fostering a culture of mutual respect can create a positive balance that enhances team morale and resilience.

The key is to make regular, intentional deposits through small, consistent actions. A heartfelt compliment, a thoughtful gesture, or a moment of undivided attention may seem insignificant, but over time these investments compound, creating an emotional safety net that allows relationships to thrive.

The text message battlefield became my next laboratory for change. When emotions rose, I used to engage fully. Each text was an attack to win. It never solved anything and always made things worse. Now when I feel the heat, I acknowledge it needs to be addressed, but I choose to sleep on it and let the emotion pass. Sleeping on things has been a monumental change. Chelsea used to do this with me, but I misinterpreted it as not feeling validated and let resentment brew until my outbursts exploded. I can't count how many times arguments escalated until the cops were called. It's sincerely embarrassing. I finally came to accept that delaying a response isn't rejection—it's wisdom. So now I can disagree with someone without instigating more problems.

The Weekly Repair practice evolved from necessity. Hiding from my shortcomings meant nothing improved. Someone once said, "Do the things you're scared of." So once a week—for me, Sunday morning, coffee in hand—I reviewed the week. Where had I fallen short? Who deserved better? The first texts were agony.

"I was short with you Tuesday. That was about my stress, not you. I'll work on that." "I committed to helping with that project and dropped the ball. No excuse. How can I make it right?" "I realize I dominated the conversation yesterday. I should have listened more."

Simple, direct, no elaborate apologies, just acknowledgment and commitment. Over time, the weekly practice became daily awareness. Sleeping on anger became standard operating procedure. Deposits started exceeding withdrawals. Each small action was a vote for the person I wanted to become.

One of the most profound lessons I've learned is the importance of giving without expecting anything in return. It's a principle I strive to live by, but it's not always easy. There have been times when I've found myself doing something kind for someone, only to later catch myself feeling resentful or disappointed when they didn't respond in the way I had hoped. In those moments, I've had to pause and reflect on my true intentions. Was I really giving freely, or was I subconsciously attaching strings to my actions?

True kindness, I've come to understand, is a gift freely given. It's not a transaction or a means of control. When we perform acts of kindness with an expectation of reciprocity or a specific outcome, we set ourselves up for disappointment and erode the very spirit of generosity.

As I built these habits, I noticed another pattern from my early oilfield days. When I was new, the expectation was that the new guy would replace the senior guy and keep working until he was the oldest person on the job. I internalized that expectation: Any time I saw someone working, I lent a hand. As I grew and learned to engage more with people, when I identified struggles, I evaluated ways I could improve the journey for them. Acts of kindness became gifts, not loans. I contributed because it's who I chose to be. The compound effect became obvious.

Two workouts became three, became five. Consistency led to physical stability, which led to mental clarity.

Weekly repairs became immediate acknowledgments. Regular repairs prevented resentment from building. Sleeping on anger became standard practice. Pausing prevented conflicts from escalating.

Deposits started exceeding withdrawals. Relationship accounts had cushion for inevitable mistakes.

None of these changes were dramatic. And that's the point. Culture isn't built through grand gestures or massive overhauls. It's built through small, repeated actions that compound over time. Miss a workout? Go the next day. Snap at someone? Acknowledge it immediately. Feel rage rising? Sleep on it. Each vote was for the person I wanted to be—not the warrior who conquered through force, but someone who built through patience. Not the man who won arguments, but someone who preserved relationships. Not perfect, but consistent.

I use mentorship a lot when it comes to building lasting change. Through the process of mentoring and being mentored, we both grow. Having an accountability partner, someone who understands your goals and can offer support and honest feedback, is invaluable. It's not about perfection or never stumbling; it's about having someone there to remind you of your commitment and to help you get back on track when you falter.

Remember, the way you do one thing is how you do all things. When you step up and decide that your values and morals are your foundation, everything else falls into place. It's not about being flawless; it's about being consistent. It's about aligning your actions with your principles, one choice at a time.

REFLECTION: Compound Interest of Character

Culture is compound interest for character. Small deposits, made consistently, grow into something larger than their sum. The two-workout week seems insignificant compared to an extreme program, but after a year the gentle approach creates someone who works out because it's who they are, while the extreme approach leaves someone recovering from burnout. The weekly repair text seems small compared to a grand apology, but after months those acknowledgments build trust, while grand apologies without change destroy it. Sleeping on anger feels weak compared to immediate response, but over time the pause creates a reputation for thoughtfulness, while immediate reactions create a reputation for volatility.

The Love Bank applies everywhere: Every workout is a deposit in your physical account. Every pause before reacting is a deposit in your emotional account. Every repair is a deposit in your relationship account. Every kept promise is a deposit in your integrity account.

When crisis comes—and it always does—you're either overdrawn or you have reserves. The difference isn't determined in the crisis; it's determined in the thousand small moments beforehand. The personal culture you build isn't what you say you'll do. It's what you actually do, repeatedly, until it becomes who you are. And who you are, consistently demonstrated, becomes the culture you create around you. Stability isn't found, it's built. And it's built through habits so small they seem insignificant, until one day you realize they've become the architecture of your entire life.

Building a culture of stability, kindness, and growth is not a destination; it's a daily practice. It's the accumulation of countless small choices, made consistently over time. It's the decision to show up, even when you don't feel like it. To pause, even when you want to react. To give, even when you're not sure you have anything left.

The beauty of this approach is that it's available to all of us, regardless of our circumstances. We don't need to wait for a grand moment of transformation or a perfect set of conditions. We can start right now, with the very next choice we make.

So start small, but start today. Choose one habit, one practice, one small way to begin building the culture you wish to see in your life. Maybe it's a daily moment of gratitude, a weekly act of kindness, or a monthly check-in with a loved one. Whatever it is, commit to it. Show up for it, day after day, even when it feels insignificant.

Because here's the secret: There are no insignificant choices. Every action, every word, every thought is a vote for the person you want to become and the life you want to create. And as you cast those votes, one by one, you'll begin to see a shift. In your relationships, in your work, in your sense of self.

You'll realize that you're not just reacting to chaos anymore. You're creating something new, something stable, something beautiful. You're building a culture of your own design.

And that, my friend, is a legacy worth leaving.

➤Describe the things you are presently doing that are building a personal culture of your own design. Identify at least one new thing that you will begin doing.

MERCY PRACTICE: Identifying and Replacing Negative Habits

Do the first item below, then the second, third, fourth, and fifth.

1. Identify a limiting habit: Reflect on a habit or thought pattern that may be holding you back from building the personal culture you desire. This could be a tendency to procrastinate, a pattern of negative self-talk, or a habit of avoiding difficult conversations. Write down this habit and the impact it has on your life.

2. Envision a positive alternative. Imagine what your life might look like if you were to replace this limiting habit with a more constructive one. What would be different? How would you feel? What kind of culture would this new habit help create? Write down your vision in as much detail as possible.

3. Design a small, daily practice. Identify one small action you can take each day to begin shifting from the old habit to the new one. This action should be specific, manageable, and consistent. For example, if you want to replace a habit of procrastination with one of proactively, your daily practice might be to tackle the most challenging task on your to-do list first thing each morning.

4. Track your progress. Create a simple way to hold yourself accountable and celebrate your consistency. This could be a habit tracker app, a journal where you record your daily practice, or a weekly check-in with an accountability partner. Notice how your momentum builds as you string together days and weeks of your new habit.

5. Embrace imperfection. Remember that change is rarely linear. There will be days when you fall back into old patterns, and that's okay. The key is to approach these moments with self-compassion and to recommit to your daily practice without judgment. Over time, you'll find that the new habit becomes more natural, and the old one loses its grip.

As you do this, don't worry too much about a goal. Focus on the process—just doing the stuff. That's where character is built and life is gradually transformed.

18
WHAT I LEAVE BEHIND

Legacy isn't a statue or a list of achievements. It's carved into scars, into quiet decisions, into apologies turned into actions. It's written in the choices we make when no one is watching and in the ways we respond to the moments that break us. Real legacy is quiet and messy. It looks like Madison's fists pounding her car seat because her father couldn't afford french fries. It sounds like Chelsea's laughter in a pasture as a bull chased us toward a cattle guard. It feels like Nodens curling into my arms, steadying me when everything else slipped through my hands. Those moments—painful, joyful and ordinary—are what I leave behind.

I've come to understand that legacy is not a fixed point or a final destination. It's a continuous unfolding, a series of choices and actions that shape the imprint we leave on the world. Each day, each interaction, each moment of self-reflection is an opportunity to contribute to that legacy, to build upon the foundation of our experiences and to chart a course for the person we want to become.

In my own journey, I've seen my understanding of legacy evolve from a narrow focus on accomplishments and accolades to a deeper appreciation for the quiet, often unseen ways we impact those around us. The legacy I seek to leave is not one of perfection or grandeur, but one of growth, resilience, and the capacity to transform pain into purpose.

As a parent, my deepest hope is that my children will not have to endure the same pain and struggles I faced in my life. The only way to achieve this is by sharing all that I have learned and the processes and tools I've developed in hopes that it will equip them to navigate their own challenges with greater ease and less resistance. This is the legacy I strive to leave—a path made a little smoother by the lessons I've learned, the wisdom I've gained, and the love I've poured into every step.

For Madison

I tried my best with what I had. Mental illness and trauma are invisible injuries. People with traumatic brain injuries can struggle with mood swings, impulse control, and judgment. None of that justifies the pain I caused, but it does explain why my love felt tangled in hurt. I see the strength you've built, and I hope someday I can earn the right to be part of your world again. Every page of this book carries you in it. Every lesson I learned came from failing you first. The french fries I couldn't buy taught me that presence matters more than provision. The silence between us taught me that love doesn't require acknowledgement; it requires consistency, even from a distance.

Through the years, I've chosen to be creative in finding ways to memorialize the lessons for you, to make them available if and when you choose. This book and the MessageToMadison.com website are both attempts to do my best at parenting, regardless of distance or time. I hope you can accept that I've done my best and that I love you dearly. There is always a chair for you at my table. No conditions, no expectations—just space held open by someone who loves you without requiring anything back.

For Chelsea

Without our time together I might never have accepted how much help I needed. You taught me that sunsets disappear in two minutes and forty-seven seconds, fleeting beauty that deserves our full attention. You taught me that love wants presence, not projects; connection, not provision. Every tool I learned in therapy, every choice to flow instead of fight, every breath taken instead of words thrown—all of that came from recognizing what I lost when I lost you. You were the mirror that showed me who I'd become, and losing you was the catalyst for becoming someone else. I hope you've found peace. I hope someone watches sunsets with you, present and whole. You deserved better than the broken man who tried to love you through his own unprocessed trauma. Thank you for the time you gave. It mattered. It changed me.

For You the Reader

Life throws mountains and monsters at all of us. Resilience is the learned ability to turn setbacks into growth by regaining emotional balance, adapting to change, and reframing problems as opportunities. I'm not writing to you from a summit. I'm halfway up the mountain, still climbing, still slipping, still discovering muscles I didn't know I had. Some days I slide backward. Some days the warrior tries to take back control. Some days I fail at every principle I've learned. But here's what I've discovered: You're stronger than your worst moment; you're more than your biggest failure; you're capable of change even when change seems impossible. The french fries you can't buy don't define you. The relationships you've destroyed don't complete your story. The trauma you've survived doesn't get the final word. Every mountain you face is climbable, even if you have to crawl. Every monster you battle teaches you something about your own strength. Every moment of mercy you extend to others and to yourself builds a bridge to who you are becoming.

This book is proof that broken people can rebuild. Fathers who fail can still love. Warriors can learn to flow. The worst parts of us may simply be our best parts misdirected. And "nobody's coming to save you" isn't a curse, it's liberation. If you realize your perspective can transform obstacles into opportunities for growth, you reclaim power over your story.

To the reader who has walked this path with me, who has seen their own struggles and triumphs reflected in these pages, I offer this invitation: Keep climbing. Keep choosing mercy, for yourself and for others. Keep believing that your story, no matter how painful or complicated, is a story worth telling.

Your mountains may be different from mine, your monsters may wear different faces, but the journey of growth and self-discovery is a path we all walk. And as you navigate the twists and turns of your own path, remember that you are never alone. Remember that each step, each stumble, each moment of doubt is a chance to learn, to adapt, to become more fully yourself.

So take the lessons of this book, the insights gleaned from my own imperfect journey, and make them your own. Use them as a compass, a guide, a reminder that even in the darkest moments, there is always a way forward. And know that as you climb, as you face your own mountains and monsters, you are leaving a legacy of your own—a legacy of courage, of resilience, and of the transformative power of mercy.

For those facing mountains that continue to stack in front of you, I hope some of the tools shared in this book can help you preserve the relationships around you. Because at the end of the day, those relationships are what truly matter, what are meant to be valued and carried through the storm. The connections we forge, the love we share, the moments of grace and understanding we extend to one another—that is the legacy that endures.

The 2:47 Sunset

Chelsea's 2:47 reminder is a compass. It says life is shorter than we think. Presence is everything. Every choice to pause instead of react matters. Every small deposit into someone's love bank matters. I've lost more than most people will ever have. Houses. Health. Marriages. Children. Dogs. Dignity. But losing everything has shown me what actually matters—not stuff, but lessons, growth and the ability to keep standing when standing seems impossible.

On the days when I've been overextended or caught in the grind, if I catch a sunset, I always try to take a moment to let it in. Something about that moment is rejuvenating to me. Furthermore, as I get older, more people that I thought would be around forever are no longer here. It's a tough pill to swallow that life truly passes in the blink of an eye. The 2:47 sunset serves as a constant reminder to be present, to prioritize what genuinely matters, and to find gratitude in the fleeting beauty of each moment.

The Final Climb

I'm still climbing. Every day. Some days it's two steps forward and three steps back. Some days I reach a new plateau. Some days I sit on a rock and cry. But I keep climbing because that's what we do. We climb. The thirty-day climb at the end of this book isn't an appendix. It's an invitation. Join me. Not because I have all the answers, but because the path is easier with company. Your mountains might be different from mine, but climbing is universal.

REFLECTION: Evidence of Standing

Legacy isn't about being flawless; it's about leaving behind evidence that you kept standing, that you kept showing up, that you turned wounds into wisdom and scars into strength. This book is my evidence. Every chapter proves that breaking doesn't mean ending; every story testifies that failures can become foundations. I may never speak to Madison again. Chelsea has certainly moved on. The people I've hurt may never know I changed. But this book stands as witness that their pain taught me. It changed me. It made me someone who can write these words for others who may be drowning in floods, trapped in fires, broken by crashes.

That's legacy—not perfection, but evolution. Not arrival, but journey. Not conquering mountains, but showing others they can climb them too. The empty chair stays empty for now. The silence continues. The climb never ends. But somewhere, someone is holding this book, seeing their own mountains and monsters reflected in mine, and realizing they're not alone. Resilience isn't about avoiding hardship; it's about harnessing it as a platform for growth. Mercy isn't weakness; it's strength under control. And love doesn't expire just because it can't be returned. That's what I leave behind—not answers, but footprints showing the redemptive path is walk able.

By sharing my story, by laying bare the wounds and the healing, the failures and the triumphs, I hope to leave a trail of footprints for others to follow. Not a path to perfection, but a path to possibility—a reminder that even in our brokenness, we have the capacity to heal, to grow, to transform our pain into something beautiful.

This memoir is also an invitation, a hand outstretched to anyone who has ever felt lost, broken, or alone. It is a reminder that our stories, no matter how messy or complicated, have the power to inspire, to comfort, and to light the way for someone else.

And so, as I look to the future and the legacy I hope to leave, I do so with a renewed sense of purpose. I may never know the full impact of my words or the ripples they may create in the lives of others. But I take solace in the knowledge that by sharing my truth, by offering my own hard-won wisdom, I am playing a small part in building a world where compassion triumphs over judgment, where healing is possible, and where every person, no matter their past, has the chance to write a new ending.

And to Madison, to Chelsea, to every person who has been a part of this journey – thank you. Thank you for the lessons, for the love, for the chance to grow. Know that you are always with me, even in the silence. Know that your impact, your presence, your heart will forever be woven into the fabric of my story.

Keep climbing, my friends. Keep choosing mercy. Keep believing in the power of your own story.

And know that you are never, ever alone.

The climb continues. The chair remains open. The sunset awaits.

➢What will you do from here? What legacy will you create? And toward that end, will you do the 30Day Climb to Calm, Connection, and Purpose?

MERCY PRACTICE: Building Your Own Culture of Deposits

By now you will hopefully be able to do all of these—or at least be on the way:

1. Start Small, stay Consistent. Choose one habit that aligns with the person you want to be—a weekly workout, a daily kindness, a nightly pause before responding. Commit to it for two weeks, then add another.
2. Visualize your accounts. Create a Love Bank list for the relationships and values that matter—physical health, emotional well-being, friendships, integrity. Each day,

write down one deposit you made in each account. Notice how small deposits accumulate.

3. Pause and sleep on it. When anger or frustration rises, tell yourself, "This needs to be addressed, but not now." Sleep on it. In the morning, reassess and respond with clarity. Over time, you'll see how many conflicts dissipate overnight.
4. Perform kindness without a ledger. Look for one person struggling and find a way to ease their load—offer a hand, listen, or simply acknowledge them. Give without expecting anything back. It's a gift, not a loan.
5. Weekly repair. Once a week, review interactions. Where did you withdraw more than you deposited? Send a simple text: Acknowledge the shortfall, accept responsibility, and commit to change. Over time, move this practice from weekly to whenever you notice it.

Small actions repeated often become who you are. Build your culture one deposit at a time.

30 Day Climb to Calm, Connection, and Purpose

Ryan Castleberry, author of

Mountains, Monsters, and Mercy: A Father's Reckoning with Loss, Grit, and the Climb Back to Grace

30 Days to Rebuild Calm, Connection and Purpose — One Breath at a Time

Every practice in this guide is rooted in research from leading medical institutions and mental health experts. Click the blue links to explore the source of each recommendation and know you're backed by science on your climb.

Introduction

When the weight feels too heavy and the world too loud, the climb begins with a single breath. The Mercy Climb isn't about perfection—it's about proof. These daily, sciencebacked practices rebuild calm, connection, and purpose in minutes. Across thirty days you'll explore mindfulness, gratitude, movement, creativity, and reflection. Each day is a small step. Together, they chart a path back to yourself.

Daily Practices Day One — Gratitude Journal

Write down three things you're grateful for today. This simple act retrains the brain to notice small positives, increasing happiness, and reducing anxiety and depression.

MERCY PRACTICE: Keep your gratitude list where you can revisit it when feeling low.

Day Two — Mindful Breathing

Spend five minutes practicing mindful breathing. Inhale slowly through your nose and exhale gently through your mouth, counting to five with each breath. Focusing on your breath calms the nervous system and brings you into the present moment.

MERCY PRACTICE: Close your eyes and place your hand on your chest as you breathe to deepen the connection.

Day Three — Nature Time

Spend at least twenty minutes outdoors in a park, garden, or near trees. Immersing yourself in nature lowers cortisol (a stress hormone) and improves mood and wellbeing.

MERCY PRACTICE: Leave your phone at home and pay attention to sights, sounds, and smells during your walk.

Day Four — Creative Expression

Engage in an art or craft activity such as drawing, painting, knitting, writing, or cooking for at least thirty minutes. Creative expression provides a sense of purpose and has a significant positive impact on happiness and wellbeing, comparable to the benefits of a job.

MERCY PRACTICE: Focus on the process rather than the outcome; let yourself play.

Day Five — Digital Detox

Take a two hour break from screens. Use this time to connect with family or friends, read a book, or enjoy a hobby. Reducing screen time improves mood, sleep, and social connections.

MERCY PRACTICE: Turn off notifications and put devices in another room to fully unplug.

Day Six — Move Your Body

Do at least thirty minutes of physical activity you enjoy—walking, running, cycling, dancing, or yoga. Aerobic exercise diverts attention from worries, releases ant anxiety petrochemicals, and builds resilience.

MERCY PRACTICE: Notice how movement shifts your mood and energy.

Day Seven — Kindness Act

Perform one random act of kindness today. Compliment a stranger, pay for someone's coffee, donate gently used items, or write a thank you note. Kindness improves happiness, reduces anxiety, increases social connectedness, and even lowers stress hormones.

MERCY PRACTICE: Reflect on how the act made you feel as well as the recipient's response.

Day Eight — Self Compassion Letter

Write a compassionate letter to yourself as if you were comforting a dear friend. Acknowledge your struggles and offer yourself encouragement and kindness. Self compassion helps reduce anxiety and depression and fosters resilience.

MERCY PRACTICE: Read your letter aloud to yourself and keep it to revisit when needed.

Day Nine — Nourishing Meal

Prepare and enjoy a meal rich in vegetables, fruits, whole grains, and lean proteins. High quality foods nourish the brain, protect it from oxidative stress, and are associated with a lower risk of depression.

MERCY PRACTICE: Notice flavors, textures, and your body's signals of fullness and satisfaction.

Day Ten — Journaling for Clarity

Spend fifteen minutes journaling your thoughts and feelings. Writing helps process emotions, breaks cycles of rumination, and reduces anxiety and depressive symptoms.

MERCY PRACTICE: Try free writing without censoring yourself; let your thoughts flow onto the page.

Day Eleven — Yoga or Stretching

Practice thirty minutes of yoga or gentle stretching. Yoga emphasizes breathing and meditation, reduces anxiety and depression, increases levels of the calming neurotransmitter GABA, and strengthens key brain regions.

MERCY PRACTICE: Use an online video or class if you're new to yoga, and remember to breathe deeply into each stretch.

Day Twelve — Social Connection

Reach out to a friend or family member for a phone call, video chat, or in person visit. Strong social connections help people live longer and reduce the risk of heart disease, stroke, anxiety, depression, and dementia.

MERCY PRACTICE: Share a favorite memory or ask a meaningful question to deepen the conversation.

Day Thirteen — Declutter a Space

Choose one small area—a drawer, shelf, or desktop—to tidy and declutter. Clearing physical clutter reduces cortisol levels, increases focus, and can improve sleep.

MERCY PRACTICE: As you let go of items, thank them for their service and notice any shift in your mood.

Day Fourteen — Positive Self Talk

Notice a negative thought and replace it with a positive or compassionate statement, such as, "I'm doing my best" or, "I am capable and resilient." Positive selftalk improves self-esteem, reduces depression and anxiety, and makes you feel more in control of your life.

MERCY PRACTICE: Write your affirmation on a sticky note and place it where you'll see it often.

Day Fifteen — Set a Goal

Identify one meaningful goal and break it down into manageable steps. Goal setting improves focus, motivation, autonomy, self-esteem, and wellbeing.

MERCY PRACTICE: Choose a small action you can take today toward your goal and schedule it in your calendar.

Day Sixteen — Reading Break

Spend twenty minutes reading a book, article, or poetry that interests you. Reading reduces stress, slows heart rate, relaxes muscles, and engages the imagination.

MERCY PRACTICE: Find a quiet, comfortable spot and allow yourself to be fully absorbed in the story.

Day Seventeen — Plan a Future Adventure

Research and plan a future trip or local excursion. Even anticipating a getaway increases happiness and provides a sense of control and excitement.

MERCY PRACTICE: Dream big or small—it could be a weekend hike, a museum visit, or a cross-country journey.

Day Eighteen — Music Therapy

Listen to or play music for twenty minutes. Music stimulates the brain, reduces anxiety, blood pressure, and pain, and improves sleep quality, mood, mental alertness, and memory.

MERCY PRACTICE: Create a playlist of songs that lift your spirit and return to it when you need a boost.

Day Nineteen — Hobby Time

Spend time on a hobby you love or try something new such as gardening, cooking, woodworking, or knitting. People with hobbies report better health, greater happiness, fewer depressive symptoms, and higher life satisfaction.

MERCY PRACTICE: Schedule regular hobby time in your week to make it a habit.

Day Twenty — Deep Breathing Reset

Practice a deep breathing exercise: inhale through your nose to a slow count of five, hold briefly, then exhale through your mouth to a count of five. Repeat for five minutes. Regular practice calms the body and mind.

MERCY PRACTICE: Use this breathing technique anytime you feel stress rising during the day.

Day Twenty-One — Priorities Sleep

Commit to a healthy sleep routine: go to bed and wake up at consistent times, create a restful environment, and avoid screens before bedtime. Quality sleep is vital for memory, concentration, and emotional processing, and it reduces worry and insomnia.

MERCY PRACTICE: Develop a calming bedtime ritual such as reading, stretching, or listening to soothing music.

Day Twenty-Two — Mindful Eating

Eat one meal slowly and mindfully. Notice the taste, smell, texture, and appearance of your food. Mindful eating helps you savor each bite, tune into hunger and fullness cues, and fosters gratitude for nourishment.

MERCY PRACTICE: Put down your utensils between bites and take a few deep breaths before starting your meal.

Day Twenty-Three — Progressive Muscle Relaxation

Spend ten-to-twenty minutes tensing and then relaxing each muscle group, starting from your toes and moving up to your head. Progressive muscle relaxation reduces stress, relieves insomnia, and eases chronic pain by promoting deep relaxation.

MERCY PRACTICE: Combine muscle relaxation with slow breathing for an even deeper sense of calm.

Day Twenty-Four — Gratitude Letter

Write a letter or email to someone who has made a difference in your life. Express your appreciation and tell them how they've impacted you. Sharing gratitude boosts both the giver's and receiver's wellbeing and reduces anxiety.

MERCY PRACTICE: If you can, read the letter aloud to the person or mail it as a surprise.

Day Twenty-Five — Photo Nature Walk

Take a walk with your camera or phone and photograph details that catch your eye—patterns, colors, textures, or landscapes. Being present in nature lowers stress and invites curiosity and creativity.

MERCY PRACTICE: Print or save your favorite photo as a reminder of your connection to the natural world.

Day Twenty-Six — Hydration and Reflection

Drink plenty of water throughout the day and reflect on how hydration fuels your body and mind. Adequate water intake supports cognitive function, mood, and energy levels.

MERCY PRACTICE: Replace one sugary beverage with water and notice how your body responds.

Day Twenty-Seven — Move in a New Way

Try a new form of movement, such as hiking, dancing, swimming, or a fitness class. Adding variety keeps exercise enjoyable and builds resilience.

MERCY PRACTICE: Invite a friend to join you and turn movement into a social activity.

Day Twenty-Eight — Dance and Music Break

Put on a favorite song and dance freely for ten minutes. Combining music and movement lifts mood, reduces stress, and releases feel good endorphins.

MERCY PRACTICE: Don't worry about how you look; focus on how you feel while moving.

Day Twenty-Nine — Vision and Reflection

Create a mini vision board or write about your hopes and goals for the future. Visualizing your desired life helps clarify priorities, enhances motivation, and keeps you aligned with your values.

MERCY PRACTICE: Revisit your vision regularly and adjust it as your goals evolve.

Day Thirty — Celebrate and Plan Ahead

Reflect on your thirty day journey, celebrate your progress, and identify practices you'd like to continue. Celebrating achievements reinforces positive habits and builds confidence for the path ahead.

MERCY PRACTICE: Share your experience with a friend or in a journal, and set an intention for how you'll carry these lessons forward.

Exercises are drawn from the book *Mountains, Monsters and Mercy by Ryan Castleberry*. Join the conversation at

#Mercy Climb and share how small daily practices are rebuilding your calm, connection, and purpose

RESOURCES MENTAL HEALTH AND CRISIS SUPPORT

If you or someone you know is struggling, please reach out. Help is available 24/7:

National Suicide Prevention Lifeline: 988 (call or text)
Available 24/7 for anyone in emotional distress or suicidal crisis

Crisis Text Line: Text HOME to 741741
Free, 24/7 support for those in crisis

National Alliance on Mental Illness (NAMI): 1-800-950-NAMI (6264), www.nami.org
Information, support, and resources for mental health

SAMHSA National Helpline: 1-800-662-HELP (4357)
Confidential, free help for substance abuse and mental health

Veterans Crisis Line: 988, then press 1
Or text 838255 for 24/7 confidential support

The Trevor Project: 1-866-488-7386
Crisis support for LGBTQ+ young people

Disaster Distress Helpline: 1-800-985-5990
For those experiencing emotional distress related to disasters

ADDITIONAL SUPPORT

Psychology Today Therapist Finder: www.psychologytoday.com
Find licensed mental health professionals in your area

Better Help: www.betterhelp.com
Online therapy and counseling services

Mental Health America: www.mhanational.org
Screening tools and resources for mental health conditions

ABOUT THE AUTHOR

Ryan Castleberry is a father, survivor, and advocate for resilience in the face of life's toughest challenges. After experiencing profound loss, financial devastation, and the depths of grief, Ryan developed the 30-Day Climb—a practical framework for rebuilding momentum through small, consistent actions.

His journey from rock bottom to grace wasn't marked by dramatic transformations or heroic moments, but by showing up day after day, choosing movement over stagnation, connection over isolation, and mercy over judgment. This is his first book.

CONNECT WITH RYAN

Visit: RyanCastleberry.com

If this book has helped you on your journey,
please consider leaving a review on Amazon.
Your story matters, and sharing it helps others find their way to the trail.
Thank you for climbing with me.

www.ingramcontent.com/pod-product-compliance
Lightning Source LLC
LaVergne TN
LVHW020719110826
845149LV00012B/2331

* 9 7 9 8 9 9 4 6 3 6 8 0 0 *